Welcoming the Holy Spirit into your Heart & Soul

Guide to an Eight Week Study of the Holy Spirit in Scripture

by

Damian and Christina Vraniak

First Published in 2018 by Waubishmaa'ingan/Whitewolf Press

Library of Congress Cataloging-in-Publication data

Vraniak, Damian A. & Christina C.
Welcoming the Holy Spirit into your Heart & Soul: Guide to an Eight-Week Study
                                        of the Holy Spirit in Scripture
    text by Damian A. and Christina C. Vraniak
        p. cm.
    Includes bibliographic references
    ISBN-13: 9780998605128 (softbound)
    ISBN-10: 0-998605128 (softbound)
        1. The Teachings of Jesus. 2. Bible Study.
        I. Vraniak, Damian A. II. Title. III. Series.
        BS2415   2018

Library of Congress Control Number: 2018909828

Printed in the USA
10 9 8 7 6 5 4 3 2 1

Dedication

Our son, *Arendaki Sage Vraniak*, will be baptized soon and we wish to dedicate this study of the Holy Spirit to him. The name, *Arendaki*, in Huron means *'Spirit of the Rock'*, comes from his great grandfather, Nicholas Arendaki, who received the Gospel and became Christian with his wife Jeanne Otriohandet, and who died protecting his family and faith in 1650, as the Iroquois destroyed the Huron Nation. His death, and the death of his wife a few years later, resulted in his daughter, granddaughter and great granddaughter being educated by Saint Marie (Guyart) and her companion Ursulines in Quebec City in the decades following his death. May *'Aren'* find upon his birth two parents who also are one in their devotion to our beloved Jesus Christ, and, with the brilliant light of His Saving Grace, may the love of our Lord come into *Arendaki* as each new day breaks upon the *Spirit of the Rock* on the little prairie and savanna along the river where we live.

Acknowledgements

We would like to offer our appreciation to Wayne and Betty Tripp, for being who they are in our lives, and to Barb and Grayson Turpin, for being who they are in the life of our son, Daybreak.

Table of Contents

Preface

This study guide focuses upon what the Bible *(NIV)* says about the *Holy Spirit*. We gathered together several couples interested in our initial study. Then Damian compiled all references to the *"Holy Spirit"* in the Bible. In the process he found that Scripture actually mentioned *'heart'* more often and subsequently looked at and compiled all the references to the *'heart'*, *'soul'*, and *'spirit*(s)*'*, in order that he and Christina and the other study participants might begin to explore the relationships between the Holy Spirit and these other important parts of being a human being and a Christian.

The effort of this study was to stay close to the Word; that is, rather than rely on the interpretations of scholars and other authors, we sought to invite the Holy Spirit directly into our hearts through study of the Word.

In the end, we spent the first four weeks studying the references in Scripture to *heart*, *soul*, *spirit*, and *demons*, respectively, each week. Then we spent a week studying references that included mentions of combinations of *heart and soul*, *body and mind*. Finally, we spent three weeks studying Biblical references to the *Spirit of God*, the *Spirit of Jesus* and the *Holy Spirit*, to see if we might more clearly discern the operations of the Holy Spirit upon our hearts, souls, bodies and minds.

The source material was assembled for our study participants, as it is for you, in three forms: The first is contained in the Appendices - it is a direct compilation of the sentences in Scripture that contain each word studied each week. The second form entailed Damian arranging those passages thematically and then sequentially, removing duplication, as well as doing some minimal editing to create a smooth narrative. This *'condensation'* was quite helpful is discerning patterns between the passages and meaningful relationships among the weekly concepts studied. Finally, it was especially helpful to us to have this condensed version broken up into negative and positive oriented passages, that is, proscriptions and warnings (don't do) and affirmations (do do) for us in our concluding week of study.

Our brief reflections are included and are only that, our reflections about what came into our hearts. We invite you to welcome the Word into your hearts and find, in your own way, such transformations akin to those we experienced in our study of the Holy Spirit in the Bible.

Introduction

In our study, we found that the heart seemed the primary and critical arena of contention. Impure spirits and demons seek to influence our hearts, and the Spirit of God, the Holy Spirit, seeks to inform and redeem those same hearts. If the heart is arena, the primary field of contention, what relation do choices of the heart have in relation to our soul, to our spirit? What treasure and trash does our heart send to our soul and spirit? What *is* our soul and how is it different from our spirit? How does the Holy Spirit seek to operate upon these aspects of our selves? Such questions are the ones we took up in this study and ask you to take up as well.

As we went along, we were struck by the perception that the passages we studied often dealt with division, separation and alienation (Hebrews 4:12 *For the word of God is alive and active. Sharper than any double-edged sword, it penetrates even to dividing soul and spirit, joints and marrow; it judges the thoughts and attitudes of the heart;* James 1:8 *Come near to God and he will come near to you. Wash your hands, you sinners, and purify your hearts, you double-minded;* Luke 8:29 *For Jesus had commanded the impure spirit to come out of the man. Many times it had seized him, and though he was chained hand and foot and kept under guard, he had broken his chains and had been driven by the demon into solitary places.*), as well as with unification (Acts 4:32 *All the believers were one in heart and mind;* 1Thessalonians 5:23 *May God himself, the God of peace, sanctify you through and through. May your whole spirit, soul and body be kept blameless at the coming of our Lord Jesus Christ*). So questions came to us about how impure and pure spirits engage our hearts, how our souls seem to record and become a repository for our choices of the heart, choices that either separate or unify us with others, with Christ, with God.

We are aware that others have taken up such questions:

Letter 118   From Quebec 1648

"... I mean to say that you should not spend too long reasoning and meditating, but when you have employed your intellect for a reasonable time let the heart take over ... by speaking and singing in your heart. To make yourself worthy of this practice, you must have great purity of heart... I would like to place you in the heart of God. You will lodge there by humility, for He is the Father of the little and humble and He carries His children in His heart." ~ Marie if the Incarnation 1599-1672 Correspondence, Translated by SR. M. St Dominic O.S.U., 1681/1971/2000, p 138)

"I salute the light within your eyes where the whole universe dwells. For when you are at that center within you and I am at that place within me, we shall be one."
~ Chief Crazy Horse, Oglala Sioux, 1877

chante ishta = 'to see with the heart' (Lakota)
muzhituming – to feel what you do not see' (Ojibwe)

"Part of the meaning of being reborn is emerging from the lodge with a newly clear mind, then continuing to think about the things one learned there. Black Elk tells of the *inipi's* leader saying: "The helper will soon open the door for the last time, and when it is open we shall see the Light. For it is the wish of *Wakan-Tanka* that the Light enters into the darkness, that we may see not only with our two eyes, but with the one eye of the heart *[Chante Ishta],* and with which we see and know all that is true and good. We give thanks to the helper; may his generations be blessed! It is good! It is finished! *Hetchetu alo!*" ~ Black Elk (Joseph Brown, 1974, p 42).

"A mind of light is a mind that has fallen to its knees before the Heart, and is open to the Silence that breathes through it." ~ Ellen Davis

"We had just finished writing up and publishing our study of the 'little stories' (parables) of Jesus that confront the hardening of hearts causing people 'to see but not perceive, to hear but not understand'. The golden thread running through the stories is how one might begin to receive and welcome with an open heart, as my distant cousins Black Elk and Crazy Horse suggest, that which is at the center and unseen, unseeable, except with the heart. It reminds me of a similar concept in Ojibwe - *muzhituming* - meaning 'to feel what you do not see'. This processing with the heart, thinking with the heart, if you will, is believed to be the portal to the soul. The little stories propose a most important sequence - 'to love with all your heart and all your soul and all your strength (body), and all your mind'. This sequence suggests that if you open and process with the heart, you may enter the space of the soul, from which the most beneficial action may be determined and proceed, with the mind bringing up the rear, only dealing with the details after the passage through the heart, soul and body." ~ Damian Vraniak, November 23, 2017

Proverbs 4:23

Above all else, guard your heart, for everything you do flows from it.

Heart (1)

Jesus as the Model for a Heart

My heart is to be pure, gentle, humble, noble and good, pondering, wondering and believing, not doubting, troubled, or afraid. My heart goes out and offers empathy and encouragement to others - treasuring, loving and forgiving - burning for greater love.

What God has Done, is Doing, will Do

Lord, you know everyone's heart. You will bring to light what is hidden in darkness and will expose the motives of my heart, laying bare the secrets of my heart.
Your love has been poured out into my heart, sent in the Spirit of your Son into my heart, purifying and opening it to the light of the knowledge of your glory. You will guard my heart, strengthen and direct my heart, putting into it that which will accomplish your purpose, written upon my heart. This is a circumcision of my heart by the Spirit.

What a Heart should not Look Like, not Do

If my heart is not right before God, there is great distress, sorrow and unceasing anguish in my heart. Cut to the heart, weeping and breaking my heart, I grow weary and lose heart ... losing heart when rebuked. If my heart does not have the love of God within, it does not see or understand what is sown therein. Good does not go into my heart but into my stomach and the evil one takes away the word that is sown, so my heart does not believe and is far from the love of Christ. So my heart worries and is weighed down with what I might eat and drink, with the anxieties of life. My heart entertains evil thoughts, stores up evil thoughts, looks lustfully and commits murder, adultery, sexual immorality, theft, false testimony, slander. Out of the mouth of my heart comes the evil that it is full of, and these detestable things are revealed. I cannot keep from setting my heart on evil things: harboring bitter envy, selfish ambition, boasting, denying the truth. Wickedness is having such thoughts in my heart - sinful desires of the heart for the sexual impurity of degrading the body with another or taking pride in what is seen rather than in what is in the heart. I say in my heart, 'Who will ascend into heaven?'

Why My Heart Might Respond in that Way

Ignorance that is in me is due to the hardening of my heart. I harden my heart as they did in the rebellion when they refused to obey, rejecting him and turning back to Egypt. Calloused and not understanding, a veil covers my heart. If my heart and ears are still uncircumcised, I resist the Holy Spirit. My heart is always going astray, not knowing the ways of the Lord. My sinful, unbelieving heart turns away from the living God. My heart condemns me, although God is greater than my heart. Satan can so fill my heart, that my foolish heart is darkened.

What God Then Does

God searches and tests my heart, judging the thoughts and attitudes of my heart. If my heart is darkened in my understanding I am separated from the life of God.

<u>The Appropriate Response of My Heart</u>
My heart reveres Christ as Lord and the peace of Christ rules in my heart. My glad and sincere heart is set on things above, and I sing to God with cheerful reverence, gratitude and joy in my heart. I call on the Lord, draw near to him, to have my heart cleansed and purified.

<u>My Heart is to Encourage Other Hearts</u>
One in heart, we open wide our hearts. As you have a place in my heart make room for me in your heart. Let us be encouraged in heart and united in love, sincerely loving one another deeply from the heart. Let God find me one after his own heart, who is his very heart. I decide in my heart to give cheerful, encouragement to other hearts, and as I refresh my heart in Christ, they will as well.

<u>I will Sustain My Heart's Response</u>
I will remain true to and obey the Lord with all my heart. Justified in doing the will of God from my heart, working at it with all my heart, I will not lose heart. The eyes of my heart will be enlightened in order that I know that Christ dwells in my heart through faith, and my heart will be strengthened by grace.

Our Reflections: In Scripture, *lebab* (Hebrew), *kardia* (Greek), *heart* (English) is the most frequently used term for the inward, innermost seat or field where emotions, feelings, affections and desires initiate inclinations, impulses, desires and intentions, which lead to what and to how we give attention, perception and understanding that affects discernment, deliberation, decision-making, volition and will. In a word and in the Bible, the *heart* is the place where *choice* is made and where the consequences for health and sickness, good and evil, the self and the sacred, are determined. While the *body* carries out these choices, and the *mind* may determine the details of how the body enacts them, it is in the field of the heart that the treasure is found or not, secured or lost.

We see that a heart may be characterized as open versus closed, unified/whole versus fragmented/divided, accepting versus rejecting, life promoting versus destructive, loving versus hateful, transparent or hidden, full of faith and grace or full of distress and despair, pure or unclean, purified or uncleansed … *As I open continually to the ever-presence of the Lord's love pouring into my heart, then, two quite different consequences occur – I am shielded from, and emptied of, worldly concerns and worries, and there is more room for that love to pour in and to pour out from and into other hearts. There is less space for evil and more space for love. I move away from being divided in despite or despair and toward being one heart unified in love. I am joined with the whole and holy love of the Father and the Son.*

Your Reflections:

Your Study Partner's Reflections:

Soul (2)

God Created the Living Soul

So God created the great creatures of the sea and every living soul with which the water teems and that moves about in it, according to their kinds, and every winged bird according to its kind. And God saw that it was good. Then the Lord God formed a man from the dust of the ground and breathed into his nostrils the breath of life, and the man became a living soul.

The Soul's *Response* to Being Alive

Awake, my soul! Awake, harp and lyre! I will awaken the dawn.
Praise the Lord, my soul; with all my inmost being, praise his holy name.
Praise the Lord, my soul, and forget not all his benefits. Praise the Lord, all his works everywhere in his dominion. Praise the Lord, my soul. Praise the Lord, my soul. Lord my God, you are very great; you are clothed with splendor and majesty. My soul glorifies the Lord.

The Soul's *Accumulating Experience* of Being Alive

So, why, my soul, are you downcast? Why so disturbed within me?
What I see brings grief to my soul. The souls of the wounded cry out for help. As a righteous man, living among them day after day, I am tormented in my righteous soul by the lawless deeds I see and hear. They say, 'Come along with us; let's lie in wait for innocent blood, let's ambush some harmless soul'; another dies in bitterness of soul, never having enjoyed anything good. My soul is weary with sorrow. My soul is in deep anguish. How long, Lord, how long? Have I not wept for those in trouble? Has not my soul grieved for the poor? Why is light given to those in misery, and life to the bitter of soul? What good will it be for me to gain the whole world, yet forfeit my soul; what can anyone give in exchange for their soul? So I abstain from sinful desires, which wage war against my soul. I loathe my very life; therefore I will give free rein to my complaint and speak out in the bitterness of my soul.
Do not take away my soul along with sinners, Lord, my life with those who are bloodthirsty. You saw my affliction and knew the anguish of my soul. I will walk humbly all my years because of this anguish of my soul. My soul is overwhelmed with sorrow to the point of death. Now my soul is troubled, and what shall I say? They will weep over me with anguish of soul and with bitter mourning.

The Soul Remembers, Hopes, Delights, and is Refreshed

My soul is consumed with longing for your laws at all times.
My soul thirsts for God, for the living God. When can I go and meet with God?
As the deer pants for streams of water, so my soul pants for you, my God.
My soul faints with longing for your salvation, but I have put my hope in your word.
March on, my soul; be strong! We have this hope as an anchor for the soul, firm and secure. It enters the inner sanctuary behind the curtain. I pour out my soul to the Lord. These things I **remember** *as I pour out my soul. A longing fulfilled is sweet to the soul.*

I delight greatly in the Lord; my soul rejoices in my God. For he has clothed me with garments of salvation and arrayed me in a robe of his righteousness, as a bridegroom adorns his head like a priest, and as a bride adorns herself with her jewels. My soul will rejoice in the Lord and delight in his salvation, for we are receiving the end result of our faith, the salvation of our souls.

The law of the Lord is perfect, refreshing the soul. He refreshes my soul. He guides me along the right paths for his name's sake. This is what the Lord says: "Stand at the crossroads and look; ask for the ancient paths, ask where the good way is, and walk in it, and you will find rest for your souls." Yes, my soul, find rest in God; my hope comes from him. Truly my soul finds rest in God; my salvation comes from him. Return to your rest, my soul, for the Lord has been good to you.

The Soul Rests

Like cold water to a weary soul is good news from a distant land. We have returned to the Shepherd and Overseer of our souls. I saw under the altar the souls of those who had been slain because of the word of God and the testimony they had maintained. And I saw the souls of those who had been beheaded because of their testimony about Jesus and because of the word of God. They had not worshiped the beast or its image and had not received its mark on their foreheads or their hands. They came to life and reigned with Christ a thousand years.

Reflections: In Scripture, *nepesh* (Hebrew), *psuche* (Greek), *soul* (English) is the term used over 750 times in the Old Testament and over 600 times in the New Testament for the sensuous appetite, passion and animating life of all living beings, including human and animals, translated half the time as *soul* and half the time as *life or living essence*. In the Bible, the *soul* is the place where the *consequences and choices* we and others make *accumulate* with respect to health or sickness, good or evil, the self or the sacred. Like the layers of sediment in rock formations of a particular place on earth, the plowed paths of a specific stream or river, the rings of an individual tree, and the condition of each human body, the *soul retains, remembers and is the primary repository and reservoir* of what has been toxic and destructive or life-promoting in our living. For the early Hebrews, as well as for most North American Indians, this *life-memory* or *life-soul* ends when that life dies.

We see that a *soul* may be characterized as full of anxiety, torment and anguish, downcast, disturbed and in despair, or full of splendor, majesty, hope and delight... *As I continually awaken to each dawn, I do not forget who created the life-force within me, and so I praise, rejoice and glorify his name. As I experience and remember the inevitable poor choices I and others make that are contrary to God's living presence, law and love, I ask for the ancient wisdom and guidance of the word, that I might walk a path of light and love, as my soul is refreshed and renewed continuously, until the soul of my living being finally comes to rest.*

Your Reflections:

Your Study Partner's Reflections:

Spirit (3)

God Forms and Places Spirit Within

The first man Adam became a living being, the last Adam, a life-giving spirit. The Spirit of God has made me and sown a natural body first. Then God formed my human spirit and caused that spirit to dwell within me. I belong to Him body and spirit and He jealously longs for that spirit that dwells within me. My human spirit is the lamp of the Lord that sheds light on my inmost being, my inner self, the unfolding beauty of a gentle and quiet spirit. The Lord puts a new spirit within me, removing my heart of stone and giving me a heart of flesh. The spirit within me, the breath of the Almighty, gives me understanding.

Impure Spirits Seek Purchase

However, I am seized, overpowered, possessed, and tormented by an impure, evil spirit, a demon. Troubled by this impure, evil spirit, I am cured, the spirit driven out with a word. When an impure spirit comes out of me, it goes through arid places seeking rest and does not find it. Then it says, 'I will return to the house (heart) I left.' Then it goes and takes seven other spirits more wicked than itself and they go in and live there. And my final condition is worse than the first. And yet, Jesus said, "I command you, come out of this man, you impure spirit and never enter him again;" and it was so. And so, I do not believe every spirit, but test the spirits to see whether they are from God, because many false prophets have gone out into the world. But every spirit that does not acknowledge Jesus is not from God. This is the spirit of the antichrist. For when we were underage, we were in slavery under the elemental spiritual forces of the world. The spiritual forces of evil in the heavenly realms include the spirit who is now at work in those who are disobedient. I died with Christ to the elemental spiritual forces of this world, yet some will abandon the faith and follow deceiving spirits and things taught by demons. God gives them a spirit of stupor, eyes that do could not see and ears that do not hear, to this very day.

Distinguish Spirits

To some the gift of distinguishing between such spirits is given. Gentiles have shared in the Jews' spiritual blessings. Through God, whom I serve in my spirit, I may impart to others some spiritual gift to make them strong, although they do not lack any spiritual gift. Indeed, praise be to the God and Father of our Lord Jesus Christ, who has blessed us in the heavenly realms with every spiritual blessing in Christ. If I pray in a tongue, my spirit prays; I will pray with my spirit, but I will also pray with my understanding; I will sing with my spirit, but I will also sing with my understanding. I watch and pray so that I will not fall into temptation; the spirit is willing, but the flesh is weak. The body without the spirit is dead.

One Spirit Joined and Unified

We have the same spirit of faith, we also believe and therefore speak; let us purify ourselves from everything that contaminates body and spirit, perfecting holiness out of reverence for God. His spirit has been refreshed by all of us. Like newborn babies, I crave pure spiritual milk, so that by it I may grow up in His salvation. The grace of our Lord Jesus Christ is with my spirit, brothers and sisters. I am present with you in spirit and my joy complete by being like-minded, having the same love, being one in spirit and of one mind. We also, like living stones, are being built into a spiritual house to be a holy priesthood, offering spiritual sacrifices acceptable to God through Jesus Christ. For the word of God is alive and active. Sharper than any double-edged sword, it penetrates even to dividing soul and spirit, joints and marrow; it judges the thoughts and attitudes of the heart. Indeed, blessed are the poor in spirit. For whoever is united with the Lord is one with him in spirit. I am devoted to the Lord in both body and spirit. Spiritual seed has been sown among us and we all eat the same spiritual food and drank the same spiritual drink; for I drink from the spiritual rock that accompanies me, and that rock is Christ. I come in love and with a gentle spirit. Even though I am not physically present, I am with you in spirit. When you are assembled and I am with you in spirit, and the power of our Lord Jesus is present.

Destination of Spirit

Who knows if the human spirit rises upward and if the spirit of the animal goes down into the earth? After you were put to death, Lord, but made alive in spirit, you went and made proclamation to the imprisoned spirits, to those who were disobedient long ago. When my spirit departs, the dust I am returns to the ground it came from, and my spirit returns to God who gave it. The realm of the dead below will be all astir to meet you, Lord, at your coming; it will rouse my departed spirit to greet you. Multitudes who sleep in the dust of the earth will awake: some to everlasting life, others to shame and everlasting contempt, judged according to human standards in regard to the body, but living according to God in regard to the spirit. When I give up my spirit, Father, into your hands I commit that spirit; Lord Jesus, receive my spirit. I pray I will not be one of the dead who live no more, whose spirits will not rise, whose memory You will wipe out. May my whole spirit, soul and body be kept blameless at your coming, my Lord, Jesus Christ. So, now, I remember my songs in the night and my spirit asks you, Lord, the Judge of all, to make perfect my righteous spirit: I submit to the Father of spirits and would live! Lord, you who make your angels spirits, please send those angels to minister my spirit, so that it will inherit salvation!

Our Reflections: In Scripture, *ruach* (Hebrew), *pneuma* (Greek), *spirit* (English) is the term used nearly 400 times in the Hebrew Old Testament and nearly 400 times in the New Testament for the breath, wind and non-material being of God, angels, demons or the inward aspect of a human being. This ethereal, evanescent, fine, airy, undivided material of spirit may come to know things, separate from the living body, be pure, impure or demonic, change shape, travel, enter and leave persons and animals. In the Bible, *spirit* is the *agency, or battling agencies*, influencing the consequences and choices we and others make in our hearts with respect to health and sickness, good and evil, the self and the sacred. We find that spirits may enable wholeness or division, acceptance or rejection, be life-promoting or destructive, loving or hateful, transparent (truthful) or hidden (deceitful), pure or unclean ... *As my spirit is present and one with the Spirit of the Father and the Son, the unfolding beauty of its gentleness and quietness, unified with other spirits with the help of ministering angels, it becomes perfectly whole and holy, in belonging to our Creator and Shepard, inheriting salvation and everlasting life.*

Your Reflections:

Your Study Partner's Reflections:

Demons *(4)*

Jesus Drove Out Demons, Curing and Healing
People brought to Jesus all the sick and demon-possessed and he cured and healed them, the violent, the blind and mute, the convulsing and suffering. He drove out the spirits without injuring the individuals with a word, but he would not let the demons speak because they knew who he was.

Demons Separate and Destroy Life
For a long time a demon-possessed man had not worn clothes or lived in a house, but had lived in the tombs. Many times it had seized him, and though he was chained hand and foot and kept under guard, he had broken his chains and had been driven by the demon into solitary places. Jesus asked him, "What is your name?" "Legion," he replied, because many demons had gone into him. A large herd of pigs was feeding there on the hillside. The demons begged Jesus to let them go into the pigs, and he gave them permission. When the demons came out of the man, they went into the pigs, and the herd rushed down the steep bank into the lake and was drowned.

Demons Divide, Jesus Honors the Father and Unites
For John the Baptist came neither eating bread nor drinking wine, and you say, 'He has a demon'. By Beelzebul, the prince of demons, Jesus is driving out demons. If Satan is divided against himself, how can his kingdom stand? But if I drive out demons by the finger of God, then the kingdom of God has come upon you. "I am not possessed by a demon," said Jesus, "but I honor my Father and you dishonor me.

Jesus Gives Authority to Drive Out Demons
When Jesus had called the Twelve together, he gave them power and authority to drive out all demons. I give you the authority to drive out demons. Freely you have received; freely give. In my name they will drive out demons. They drove out many demons. Some Jews who went around driving out evil spirits tried to invoke the name of the Lord Jesus over those who were demon-possessed. We saw someone driving out demons in your name we saw someone driving out demons. They would say, "In the name of the Jesus whom Paul preaches, I command you to come out."

Demons Cannot Separate Us From Christ's Love
Neither death nor life, neither angels nor demons, neither the present nor the future, nor any powers, neither height nor depth, nor anything else in all creation, will be able to separate us from the love of God that is in Christ Jesus our Lord. You cannot drink the cup of the Lord and the cup of demons too; you cannot have a part in both the Lord's table and the table of demons. The Spirit clearly says that in later times some will abandon the faith and follow deceiving spirits and things taught by demons. You believe that there is one God. Good! Even the demons believe that—and shudder. Such "wisdom" does not come down from heaven but is earthly, unspiritual, demonic. They are demonic spirits that perform signs, and they go out to the kings of the whole world, to gather them for the battle on the great day of God Almighty. 'Fallen! Fallen is Babylon the Great!' She

has become a dwelling for demons and a haunt for every impure spirit, a haunt for every unclean bird, a haunt for every unclean and detestable animal.

Our Reflections: In Scripture, *shedim* (Hebrew), *daimon* (Greek) and *demon* (English) is mentioned 82 times in the New Testament.

With a word demons were driven out of a person without harming that person, often a person who was mute, who could not hear, and/or was blind, who could not see. What spirit is in a word that has such power, to so effect a cleansing of suffering within a person who cannot hear or see that word!?

It is clear that demons sought to shut a person off from the rest of the world, from the rest of humanity, often driving him or her to desolate places, apart from the loving communication and care of others. While seeking community (asking to be placed into a herd of pigs) themselves, demons inevitably drove the humanity they entered into desolation, despair and destruction, if the demons, themselves, were not cast out.

Possession by demons was an internal division, a house divided against itself that could not be a whole and healthy home for the heart, but only a haunt for that destined to dissolve into nothingness, eventually.

... as I suffer and cry out in the darkness of the room of my self, I push and shove upon the door to get out, but it does not move, and so I cry out to that which is outside the door of my darkness. And a voice stirs my heart and moves my hand to open the door inward, into myself ... and the light of pure spirit comes streaming in. The darkness dissipates for there is only light, it is whole and indivisible, and the darkness cannot abide in such brilliant wholiness.

Your Reflections:

Your Study Partner's Reflections:

Heart and Soul and Spirit (5)

<u>A Broken Heart Accompanied by a Double-Mind Gives the Spirit Anguish</u>
My obstinate and disloyal heart, crying out in dismay and anguish, grieves and melts with fear, as its embittered spirit grows faint with its stubborn prostitution and faithlessness, that consulting the spirits of the dead will not change. Such a troubled and anguished spirit glides into a body whose hair stands on end, disturbing the mind, and offering bitterness of soul. An uncircumcised heart that Satan has filled with the hardness of flint does not listen, but resists and lies to the Holy Spirit. Such a cunning yet despairing heart is accompanied by an anxious, cunning and disturbed double-mind. So it is that the grieving body is drenched with repulsive fruit, with the mind of an animal, and in such grieving, the sin of the soul loathes the choicest meal.

<u>A Contrite Heart Renews the Spirit and Gives Life and Rest to the Body</u>
My broken, contrite, meditating, steadfast heart (and flesh) yearns, faints and cries out for the living God to revive such a heart with the gladness, rest and peace of a gentle and humble rule, as the sacrifice of a broken and lowly spirit is renewed to steadfastness within me, and my soul makes music and sings, finding that rest, as life is given to my body and that one body rests secure, called to peace.

<u>God Reveals and Gives a New Heart and Spirit, as One</u>
The righteous God probes, searches, examines and judges the attitudes of our hearts and minds, knowing and revealing with the mind of the Spirit what we are thinking in our hearts, penetrating even to dividing soul and spirit. Yet, what is concealed in such a heart and mind is searched out, examined, probed, tested and judged. He will remove our heart of stone and give us an undivided heart of flesh, putting His laws in the hearts and minds of all believers, so that we will have a new heart and new spirit, and we will be like-minded, all of one heart and mind and spirit.

<u>We are Baptized, Purified of What Contaminates, Living with the Spirit</u>
We will devote ourselves and belong to the Lord in both body and spirit. We are all baptized by one Spirit, being sown as a natural body yet raised as a spiritual body, so that there is only one body and Spirit, purifying what contaminates the body and Spirit, so that being judged according to the body but living in regard to the Spirit. He will give us His plans and all that the Spirit may put in our mind. With this in mind, we will be alert, always praying for all of the Lord's people, that the peace of God will guard our hearts and minds in Christ Jesus.

<u>We Enter a New Covenant to Love our God with all of our heart, soul, strength and mind</u>
So it is that we enter into a covenant to love our God and to seek to love, fear, obey, serve, follow, turn and return to him, holding fast to keep his commands, statutes and decrees, in accordance with all the Law of Moses, watching and knowing, how we live and walk faithfully before him, devoting and praying to him toward the land, **with all of our heart and with all our soul, and with all our strength and mind,** *and so live,*

loving our neighbor as ourselves. May God himself, the God of peace, sanctify us through and through; may our whole spirit, soul and body be kept blameless at the coming of our Lord Jesus Christ.

Our Reflections:

Heart and Soul =   30 passages   [0 neg;   0%]

Heart and Spirit -   28 passages   [12 neg; 38%]

Heart and Mind =   20 passages   [8 neg;   40%]

Heart and Body =   6 passages   [3 neg: 50%]

Body and Spirit =   13 passages   [4 neg; 31%]

Mind and Spirit =   9 passages   [5 neg; 56%]

Soul and Spirit =   3 passages   [2 neg: 66%]

Body and Soul =   5 passages   [4 neg; 80%]

Body and Mind =   1 passages   [1 neg; 100%]

Soul and ????   =   37 Total passages   [6 neg: 16%]

Heart and ????   =   80 Total passages   [23 neg: 29%]

Spirit and ???? =   53 Total passages   [21 neg: 40%]

Body and ????   =   25 Total passages   [11 neg: 44%]

Mind and ????   =   30 Total passages   [14 neg: 47%]

Re-read the condensed version of the verses from the Old and New Testaments (100 passages), concerning various pairings of *heart and soul, heart and spirit, heart and mind*. Consider the following questions:

1. How does the *heart* seem to be the central location (arena or field) for negative and positive action and outcome?

2. How do *spirits* function as primary divine agents, affecting the heart?

3. How does the soul appear to accumulate what happens within the heart, acting as a sort of reservoir or repository, as negative and positive spirits have their effects?

4. How does the *mind* seem to function primarily as a secondary agent of negative and positive spirit?

5. How does *body* seem to reflect the general and final outcomes or products of *spirit*ual activity within the heart?

6. If the *heart* is the primary 'house' within which negative and positive *spirit*ual agents battle, and if the *soul* accumulates the results of those conflicts over time, why and how do the body and mind become 'followers' in the action, generally reflecting a 'go along' position with whomever is dominant in the *heart* at the moment?

7. What seems to be the function of division and 'oneness' in the transactions among heart, soul, spirit, body and mind? Why would you want or have to 'divide *soul* from *spirit*'?

8. How and why might the *sequence* suggested by both Moses and Jesus (*love God with all of your heart and with all your soul, and with all your strength and mind*) reflect God's guidance in how to go about making the heart, soul, body and mind *one* in loving God and our neighbor?

+ Make notes during the course of your study of these passages and summary condensations.

+ Mid-week discuss your thoughts with your study partner for the week.

+ Decide on one or two 'gems' or 'pearls' that came out of your discussion.

+ Decide which one of you will represent your pair and share the pearl(s) or gem(s) when the entire small group meets next.

What comes into the soul is at the mercy of choices made in and by the heart, as they are enacted by the body and mind. If these choices are swayed by impure spirits and demons, the trash and detritus of despair accumulate, and if these choices are informed by pure spirit and holiness, the treasures of the kingdom of heaven are granted. And in this balance the soul is bound and buried in a living death, or, upraised and uplifted into heavenly realms of the spirit. So the soul yearns to become one with spirit, for heart and soul to be united in this yearning, and for the body and mind live out such holy unification.

… and so I stop letting man-made toxins and pollutants come into the water that is the river of my life and let, no welcome, the Creator's spring and creation's rain wash clean all within my banks, so that through my life flows loving abundance, shared in unity with my brothers and sisters, human and non-human, spirit and angel.

Your Reflections:

Your Study Partner's Reflections:

The Spirit of God *(6)*

I am made by the Spirit of God
Spirit of God was hovering over the waters. The Spirit of God has made me; the breath of the Almighty gives me life.

I have rebelled against the Spirit of God
They rebelled against the Spirit of God, and rash words came from Moses' lips. How much more severely do you think someone deserves to be punished who has insulted the Spirit of grace? These are the words of him who holds the seven spirits of God and the seven stars. I know your deeds; you have a reputation of being alive, but you are dead.

The Spirit of God descended and reveals His love to me through His Son
The Holy Spirit will come on you, and the power of the Most High will overshadow you. So the holy one to be born will be called the Son of God. He saw the Spirit of God descending like a dove and alighting on him who through the Spirit of holiness was appointed the Son of God in power by his resurrection from the dead: Jesus Christ our Lord. He who searches our hearts knows the mind of the Spirit, because the Spirit intercedes for God's people in accordance with the will of God. By the power of signs and wonders, through the power of the Spirit of God, by our Lord Jesus Christ and by the love of the Spirit, to join me in my struggle by praying to God for me. These are the things God has revealed to us by his Spirit. The Spirit searches all things, even the deep things of God. God of our Lord Jesus Christ, the glorious Father, may give you the Spirit of wisdom and revelation, so that you may know him better.

Sanctified and obedient by the Spirit of God in Jesus Christ, grace and peace are mine
I ask, does God give you his Spirit and work miracles among you by the works of the law, or by your believing what you heard? God chose you as first fruits to be saved through the sanctifying work of the Spirit and through belief in the truth. Through the sanctifying work of the Spirit, to be obedient to Jesus Christ and sprinkled with his blood: Grace and peace be yours in abundance. The Spirit of glory and of God rests on you. This is how you can recognize the Spirit of God: Every spirit that acknowledges that Jesus Christ has come in the flesh is from God,
We are from God, and whoever knows God listens to us; but whoever is not from God does not listen to us. This is how we recognize the Spirit of truth and the spirit of falsehood.

I am led by the Spirit of God, as a child of God, in the realm of the Spirit
A person is a Jew who is one inwardly; and circumcision is circumcision of the heart, by the Spirit, not by the written code. Such a person's praise is not from other people, but from God. You, however, are not in the realm of the flesh but are in the realm of the Spirit, if indeed the Spirit of God lives in you. And if anyone does not have the Spirit of Christ, they do not belong to Christ. For those who are led by the Spirit of God are the children of God. For who knows a person's thoughts except their own spirit within them? In the same way no one knows the thoughts of God except the Spirit of God. What we have received is not the spirit of the world, but the Spirit who

is from God, so that we may understand what God has freely given us. The person without the Spirit does not accept the things that come from the Spirit of God but considers them foolishness, and cannot understand them because they are discerned only through the Spirit. But you were washed, you were sanctified, you were justified in the name of the Lord Jesus Christ and by the Spirit of our God. I think that I too have the Spirit of God. You are a letter from Christ, the result of our ministry, written not with ink but with the Spirit of the living God, not on tablets of stone but on tablets of human hearts. God sent the Spirit of his Son into our hearts, the Spirit who calls out, "Abba, Father."

The Spirit of God Lifts me up

He stretched out what looked like a hand and took me by the hair of my head. The Spirit lifted me up between earth and heaven and in visions of God he took me to Jerusalem, to the entrance of the north gate of the inner court, where the idol that provokes to jealousy stood. Then the Spirit lifted me up and brought me to the gate of the house of the Lord that faces east. The Spirit lifted me up and brought me to the exiles in Babylonia in the vision given by the Spirit of God. He carried me away in the Spirit to a mountain great and high, and showed me the Holy City, Jerusalem, coming down out of heaven from God.

The Spirit of God comes upon me and I speak the words of God (in prophesy)

The Spirit of God came on him ... on Amasai, chief of the Thirty, and he said: "We are yours, David!; on Saul's men; on Azariah; on Zechariah son of Jehoiada the priest. He stood before the people and said, This is what God says; and he walked along prophesying. Worship God! For it is the Spirit of prophecy who bears testimony to Jesus. For the one whom God has sent speaks the words of God, for God gives the Spirit without limit. You are praising God in the Spirit.

I am filled with the Spirit of God, with wisdom and understanding, stirred to do the works of God

He gave him the plans of all that the Spirit had put in his mind. I have filled him with the Spirit of God, with wisdom, with understanding, with knowledge and with all kinds of skills. I know that the spirit of the holy gods is in you, and no mystery is too difficult for you. Here is my dream; interpret it for me. There is a man in your kingdom who has the spirit of the holy gods in him. In the time of your father he was found to have insight and intelligence and wisdom like that of the gods. I have heard that the spirit of the gods is in you and that you have insight, intelligence and outstanding wisdom. The Lord stirred up the spirit of Zerubbabel son of Shealtiel, governor of Judah, and the spirit of Joshua son of Jozadak, the high priest, and the spirit of the whole remnant of the people. They came and began to work on the house of the Lord Almighty, their God.

I am saved and delivered by the provision of the Spirit of Jesus Christ into eternity

Take the helmet of salvation and the sword of the Spirit, which is the word of God, no one can enter the kingdom of God unless they are born of water and the Spirit. I know that through your prayers and God's provision of the Spirit of Jesus Christ what has happened to me will turn out for my deliverance. The blood of Christ, who through the eternal Spirit offered himself unblemished to God, cleanse our consciences from acts that lead to death, so that we may serve the living God! Whoever has ears, let them hear what the Spirit says to the churches. To the one who is victorious, I will give the right to eat from the tree of life, which is in the paradise of God.

Reflections: In Scripture, *Ruach Elohim*(Hebrew), *Pneuma tou Thoeu* (Greek), *Spirit of God* (English) is mentioned 31 (of 100) times and the Spirit of Jesus 2 (of 20) times in the New Testament.

I am made by the Spirit of God. I have rebelled against the Spirit of God. The Spirit of God descended and reveals His love to me through His Son. Sanctified and obedient by the Spirit of God in Jesus Christ, grace and peace are mine. I am led by the Spirit of God, as a child of God, in the realm of the Spirit. The Spirit of God Lifts me up. The Spirit of God comes upon me and I speak the words of God (in prophesy). I am filled with the Spirit of God, with wisdom and understanding, stirred to do the works of God. I am saved and delivered by the provision of the Spirit of Jesus Christ into eternity.

Your Reflections:

Your Study Partner's Reflections:

Holy Spirit *(7)*
(27 passages in the Gospels)

Conceived, Carried and Confirmed by the Holy Spirit

She was found to be pregnant through the Holy Spirit. What is conceived in her is from the Holy Spirit. The angel answered, "The Holy Spirit will come on you, and the power of the Most High will overshadow you. So the holy one to be born will be called the Son of God. When Elizabeth heard Mary's greeting, the baby leaped in her womb, and Elizabeth was filled with the Holy Spirit. He will be filled with the Holy Spirit even before he is born. Zechariah was filled with the Holy Spirit and prophesied ... the Holy Spirit was on him. It had been revealed to him by the Holy Spirit that he would not die before he had seen the Lord's Messiah. And the Holy Spirit descended on him in bodily form like a dove. And a voice came from heaven: "You are my Son, whom I love; with you I am well pleased." Jesus, full of the Holy Spirit, left the Jordan and was led by the Spirit into the wilderness,

Baptizing with the Holy Spirit

He will baptize you with the Holy Spirit and fire. He will baptize you with the Holy Spirit. He will baptize you with the Holy Spirit and fire. The man on whom you see the Spirit come down and remain is the one who will baptize with the Holy Spirit.

Giving the Holy Spirit

At that time Jesus, full of joy through the Holy Spirit, said, "I praise you, Father, Lord of heaven and earth, because you have hidden these things from the wise and learned, and revealed them to little children. Yes, Father, for this is what you were pleased to do. If you then, though you are evil, know how to give good gifts to your children, how much more will your Father in heaven give the Holy Spirit to those who ask him!" If you love me, keep my commands. The Advocate, the Holy Spirit, whom the Father will send in my name, will teach you all things and will remind you of everything I have said to you. When the Advocate comes, whom I will send to you from the Father—the Spirit of truth who goes out from the Father—he will testify about me. And with that he breathed on them and said, Receive the Holy Spirit.

Speaking of and by the Holy Spirit

David himself, speaking by the Holy Spirit, declared ... Just say whatever is given you at the time, for it is not you speaking, but the Holy Spirit. The Holy Spirit will teach you at that time what you should say. Anyone who speaks against the Holy Spirit will not be forgiven, either in this age or in the age to come. Whoever blasphemes against the Holy Spirit will never be forgiven; they are guilty of an eternal sin. Go and make disciples of all nations, baptizing them in the name of the Father and of the Son and of the Holy Spirit.

Holy Spirit (after the Gospels – 65 passages)

The Holy Spirit Testifies and Instructs

God anointed Jesus of Nazareth with the Holy Spirit and power, and he went around doing good and healing all who were under the power of the devil, because God was with him. For by one sacrifice he has made perfect forever those who are being made holy. The Holy Spirit also testifies to us about this. This is the covenant I will make with them after that time, says the Lord. I will put my laws in their hearts, and I will write them on their minds. Until the day he was taken up to heaven, after giving instructions through the Holy Spirit to the apostles he had chosen. In a few days you will be baptized with the Holy Spirit. You will receive power when the Holy Spirit comes on you and you will be my witnesses in Jerusalem, and in all Judea and Samaria, and to the ends of the earth. All of them were filled with the Holy Spirit and began to speak in other tongues as the Spirit enabled them. For prophecy never had its origin in the human will, but prophets, though human, spoke from God as they were carried along by the Holy Spirit.
They chose Stephen, a man full of faith and of the Holy Spirit; also Philip, Procorus, Nicanor, Timon, Parmenas, and Nicolas from Antioch, a convert to Judaism. Stephen, full of the Holy Spirit, looked up to heaven and saw the glory of God, and Jesus standing at the right hand of God.

Receive the Gift of the Holy Spirit

Brothers and sisters, the Scripture had to be fulfilled in which the Holy Spirit spoke long ago through David concerning Judas, who served as guide for those who arrested Jesus. Exalted to the right hand of God, he has received from the Father the promised Holy Spirit and has poured out what you now see and hear. Peter replied, repent and be baptized, every one of you, in the name of Jesus Christ for the forgiveness of your sins. And you will receive the gift of the Holy Spirit . Then Peter, filled with the Holy Spirit, said to them: You spoke by the Holy Spirit through the mouth of your servant, our father David. After they prayed, the place where they were meeting was shaken. And they were all filled with the Holy Spirit and spoke the word of God boldly. We are witnesses of these things, and so is the Holy Spirit, whom God has given to those who obey him. They prayed for the new believers there that they might receive the Holy Spirit. Because the Holy Spirit had not yet come on any of them; they had simply been baptized in the name of the Lord Jesus. Then Peter and John placed their hands on them, and they received the Holy Spirit. Give me also this ability so that everyone on whom I lay my hands may receive the Holy Spirit. While Peter was still speaking these words, the Holy Spirit came on all who heard the message. The circumcised believers who had come with Peter were astonished that the gift of the Holy Spirit had been poured out even on Gentiles. Surely no one can stand in the way of their being baptized with water. They have received the Holy Spirit just as we have. As I began to speak, the Holy Spirit came on them as he had come on us at the beginning. I remembered what the Lord had said: 'John baptized with water, but you will be baptized with the Holy Spirit.' He was a good man, full of the Holy Spirit and faith, and a great number of people were brought to the Lord. "Did you receive the Holy Spirit when you believed?" They answered, "No, we have not even heard that there is a Holy Spirit." When Paul placed his hands on them, the Holy Spirit came on them, and they spoke in tongues and prophesied. God also testified to it by signs, wonders and various miracles, and by gifts of the Holy Spirit distributed according to his will. As the Holy Spirit says: "Today, if you hear his voice, ..."

Lying to the Holy Spirit is Death

Then Peter said, "Ananias, how is it that Satan has so filled your heart that you have lied to the Holy Spirit and have kept for yourself some of the money you received for the land? You stiff-necked people! Your hearts and ears are still uncircumcised. You are just like your ancestors: You always resist the Holy Spirit! Therefore, I want you to know that no one who is speaking by the Spirit of God says, "Jesus be cursed," and no one can say, "Jesus is Lord," except by the Holy Spirit.

The Holy Spirit Chooses and Sends Those

Placing his hands on Saul, he said, "Brother Saul, the Lord—Jesus, who appeared to you on the road as you were coming here—has sent me so that you may see again and be filled with the Holy Spirit." While they were worshiping the Lord and fasting, the Holy Spirit said, "Set apart for me Barnabas and Saul for the work to which I have called them." The two of them, sent on their way by the Holy Spirit, went down to Seleucia and sailed from there to Cyprus. Then Saul, who was also called Paul, filled with the Holy Spirit, looked straight at Elymas .... It was revealed to them that they were not serving themselves but you, when they spoke of the things that have now been told you by those who have preached the gospel to you by the Holy Spirit sent from heaven. Even angels long to look into these things.

The Holy Spirit Encourages, Sanctifies and Enlightens

Living in the fear of the Lord and encouraged by the Holy Spirit, it increased in numbers. And the disciples were filled with joy and with the Holy Spirit. God, who knows the heart, showed that he accepted them by giving the Holy Spirit to them, just as he did to us. It seemed good to the Holy Spirit and to us not to burden you with anything beyond the following requirements: Keep watch over yourselves and all the flock of which the Holy Spirit has made you overseers. Be shepherds of the church of God, which he bought with his own blood. So that the Gentiles might become an offering acceptable to God, sanctified by the Holy Spirit. And you also were included in Christ when you heard the message of truth, the gospel of your salvation. When you believed, you were marked in him with a seal, the promised Holy Spirit. Anyone who rejects this instruction does not reject a human being but God, the very God who gives you his Holy Spirit. It is impossible for those who have once been enlightened, who have tasted the heavenly gift, who have shared in the Holy Spirit .... You, dear friends, by building yourselves up in your most holy faith and praying in the Holy Spirit ....

The Holy Spirit Discloses, Reveals and Gives Joy

Paul and his companions traveled throughout the region of Phrygia and Galatia, having been kept by the Holy Spirit from preaching the word in the province of Asia. I only know that in every city the Holy Spirit warns me that prison and hardships are facing me. The Holy Spirit says, 'In this way the Jewish leaders in Jerusalem will bind the owner of this belt and will hand him over to the Gentiles.'" do not grieve the Holy Spirit of God, with whom you were sealed for the day of redemption. The Holy Spirit was showing by this that the way into the Most Holy Place had not yet been disclosed. The Holy Spirit spoke the truth to your ancestors when he said through Isaiah the prophet. Our gospel came to you not simply with words but also with power, with the Holy Spirit and deep conviction. You welcomed the message in the midst of severe suffering with the joy given by the Holy Spirit.

The Holy Spirit Guards Fellowship, Pours in God's Love, Washes Rebirth and Renewal

And hope does not put us to shame, because God's love has been poured out into our hearts through the Holy Spirit, who has been given to us. I speak the truth in Christ—I am not lying, my conscience confirms it through the Holy Spirit— in purity, understanding, patience and kindness; in the Holy Spirit and in sincere love; May the grace of the Lord Jesus Christ, and the love of God, and the fellowship of the Holy Spirit be with you all. Guard the good deposit that was entrusted to you— guard it with the help of the Holy Spirit who lives in us. For the kingdom of God is not a matter of eating and drinking, but of righteousness, peace and joy in the Holy Spirit. May the God of hope fill you with all joy and peace as you trust in him, so that you may overflow with hope by the power of the Holy Spirit. He saved us through the washing of rebirth and renewal by the Holy Spirit. Your bodies are temples of the Holy Spirit, who is in you, whom you have received from God? You are not your own.

Our Reflections: In Scripture, *Ruach HoKodesh* (Hebrew), *parakletos* (Greek), *Holy Spirit* (English) is mentioned 65 times.

Jesus, the Son of God, conceived, carried and confirmed by the Holy Spirit, baptized with the Holy Spirit, gives out the Holy Spirit, speaking of and by the Holy Spirit. The Holy Spirit testifies and Instructs. Receive the gift of the Holy Spirit.
Lying to the Holy Spirit is death. The Holy Spirit chooses and sends those. The Holy Spirit encourages, sanctifies and enlightens. The Holy Spirit discloses, reveals and gives joy. The Holy Spirit guards fellowship, pours in God's love, washes rebirth and renewal.

Your Reflections:

Your Study Partner's Reflections:

The Sacred Circle: *Bible Passages Containing Heart, Soul, Body & Mind*

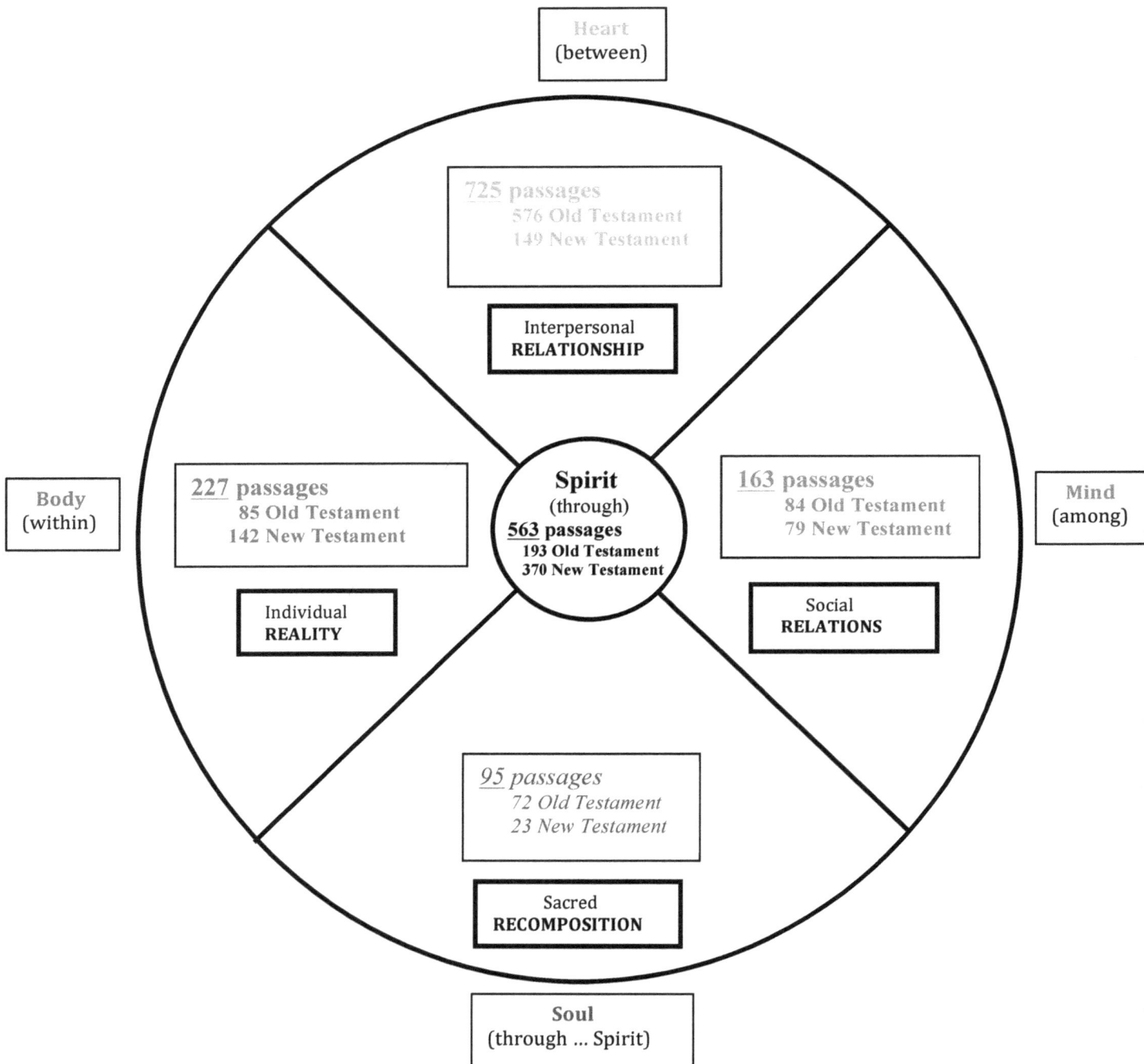

Heart
(between)

725 passages
576 Old Testament
149 New Testament

Interpersonal
RELATIONSHIP

Body
(within)

227 passages
85 Old Testament
142 New Testament

Individual
REALITY

Spirit
(through)
563 passages
193 Old Testament
370 New Testament

163 passages
84 Old Testament
79 New Testament

Social
RELATIONS

Mind
(among)

95 passages
72 Old Testament
23 New Testament

Sacred
RECOMPOSITION

Soul
(through ... Spirit)

Heart + Soul/Spirit/Mind/Body = 88 passages (all other combinations = 29 passages)

The Heart

The heart that is pure is gentle, humble, noble and good, ponders and wonders but does not doubt, is not troubled, nor afraid, rather it believes. Such a heart goes out and offers empathy and encouragement to others - treasuring, loving and forgiving. It burns for a greater love. Be encouraged in heart and united in love, that is, have sincere love for each other; love one another deeply from the heart. Let God testify that he found a person after his own heart, who is his very heart.

The heart that does not have the love of God within it does not see or understand what is sown therein. Good does not go into their hearts but into their stomachs and the evil one takes away the word that is sown, so these hearts do not believe and are far from the love of Christ. So such hearts worry and are weighed down with they what they might eat and drink, with the anxieties of life. These hearts entertain evil thoughts, store up evil thoughts. A sinful, unbelieving heart turns away from the living God. Satan can so fill your heart, that such a foolish heart is darkened. Keep us from setting our hearts on evil things: harboring bitter envy, selfish ambition, boasting, denying the truth.

The Soul

Praise the Lord, my soul; with all my inmost being, praise his holy name. Praise the Lord, my soul, and forget not all his benefits. Praise the Lord, all his works everywhere in his dominion. Praise the Lord, my soul. Praise the Lord, my soul. Lord my God, you are very great; you are clothed with splendor and majesty. My soul glorifies the Lord. The law of the Lord is perfect, refreshing the soul. He refreshes my soul. He guides me along the right paths for his name's sake. This is what the Lord says: "Stand at the crossroads and look; ask for the ancient paths, ask where the good way is, and walk in it, and you will find rest for your souls." Yes, my soul, find rest in God; my hope comes from him. Truly my soul finds rest in God; my salvation comes from him. Return to your rest, my soul, for the Lord has been good to you.

What I see brings grief to my soul. The souls of the wounded cry out for help. That righteous man, living among them day after day, was tormented in his righteous soul by the lawless deeds he saw and heard. They say, "Come along with us; let's lie in wait for innocent blood, let's ambush some harmless soul; another dies in bitterness of soul, never having enjoyed anything good. My soul is weary with sorrow. My soul is in deep anguish. How long, Lord, how long? Have I not wept for those in trouble? Has not my soul grieved for the poor? Why is light given to those in misery, and life to the bitter of soul? What good will it be for someone to gain the whole world, yet forfeit their soul; what can anyone give in exchange for their soul?

The Spirit

The first man Adam became a living being; the last Adam, a life-giving spirit. The spiritual did not come first, but the natural, and after that the spiritual. The body without the spirit is dead. It is sown a natural body, it is raised a spiritual body. If there is a natural body, there is also a spiritual body. It should be that of your inner self, the unfading beauty of a gentle and quiet spirit, which is of great worth in God's sight. Live according to God in regard to the spirit. For the word of God is alive and active. Sharper than any double-edged sword, it penetrates even to dividing soul and spirit, joints and marrow; it judges the thoughts and attitudes of the heart. May your whole spirit, soul and body be kept blameless at the coming of our Lord Jesus Christ. He makes his angels spirits, and his servants flames of fire. Are not all angels ministering spirits sent to serve those who will inherit salvation? There are spirits of the righteous made perfect, the seven spirits before God's throne, and the Lamb had seven horns and seven eyes, which are the seven spirits of God sent out into all the earth. We submit to the Father of spirits and live!

When we were underage, we were in slavery under the elemental spiritual forces of the world. The spiritual forces of evil in the heavenly realms include the spirit who is now at work in those who are disobedient. You died with Christ to the elemental spiritual forces of this world, yet some will abandon the faith and follow deceiving spirits and things taught by demons. God gave them a spirit of stupor, eyes that could not see and ears that could not hear, to this very day. Do not believe every spirit, but test the spirits to see whether they are from God, because many false prophets have gone out into the world. But every spirit that does not acknowledge Jesus is not from God. This is the spirit of the antichrist. The Spirit clearly says that in later times some will abandon the faith and follow deceiving spirits and things taught by demons. You believe that there is one God. Good! Even the demons believe that—and shudder.

Relationship Among Heart, Soul and Spirit (Body and Mind)

My broken, contrite, meditating, steadfast heart (and flesh) yearns, faints and cries out for the living God to revive such a heart with the gladness, rest and peace of a gentle and humble rule, as the sacrifice of a broken and lowly spirit is renewed to steadfastness within me, and my soul makes music and sings, finding that rest, as life is given to my body and that one body rests secure, called to peace. The righteous God probes, searches, examines and judges the attitudes of our hearts and minds, knowing and revealing with the mind of the Spirit what we are thinking in our hearts, penetrating even to dividing soul and spirit. He will remove our heart of stone and give us an undivided heart of flesh, putting His laws in the hearts and minds of all believers, so that we will have a new heart and new spirit, and we will be like-minded, all of one heart and mind and spirit. So it is that we enter into a covenant to love our God and to seek to love, fear, obey, serve, follow, turn and return to him, holding fast to keep his commands, statutes and decrees, in accordance with all the Law of Moses, watching and knowing, how we live and walk faithfully before him, devoting and praying to him toward the land, **with all of our heart and with all our soul, and with all our strength and mind,** *and so live, loving our neighbor as ourselves*

My obstinate and disloyal heart, crying out in dismay and anguish, grieves and melts with fear, as its embittered spirit grows faint with its stubborn prostitution and faithlessness, that consulting the spirits of the dead will not change. Such a troubled and anguished spirit glides into a body whose hair stands on end, disturbing the mind, and offering bitterness of soul. An uncircumcised heart that Satan has filled with the hardness of flint does not listen, but resists and lies to the Holy Spirit. Such a cunning yet despairing heart is accompanied by an anxious, cunning and disturbed double-mind. Yet, what is concealed in such a heart and mind is searched out, examined, probed, tested and judged. So it is that the grieving body is drenched with repulsive fruit, with the mind of an animal, and in such grieving, the sin of the soul loathes the choicest meal.

The Spirit of God

The Spirit of God was hovering over the waters. The Spirit of God has made me; the breath of the Almighty gives me life. He who searches our hearts knows the mind of the Spirit, because the Spirit intercedes for God's people in accordance with the will of God. By the power of signs and wonders, through the power of the Spirit of God, by our Lord Jesus Christ and by the love of the Spirit. This is how you can recognize the Spirit of God: Every spirit that acknowledges that Jesus Christ has come in the flesh is from God. We are from God, and whoever knows God listens to us; but whoever is not from God does not listen to us. This is how we recognize the Spirit of truth and the spirit of falsehood. You, however, are not in the realm of the flesh but are in the realm of the Spirit, if indeed the Spirit of God lives in you. And if anyone does not have the Spirit of Christ, they do not belong to Christ. For those who are led by the Spirit of God are the children of God. For who knows a person's thoughts except their own spirit within them? In the same way no one knows the thoughts of God except the Spirit of God. What we have received is not the spirit of the world, but the Spirit who is from God, so that we may understand what God has freely given us. The person without the Spirit does not accept the things that come from the Spirit of God but considers them foolishness, and cannot understand them because they are discerned only through the Spirit. Take the helmet of salvation and the sword of the Spirit, which is the word of God, no one can enter the kingdom of God unless they are born of water and the Spirit.

They rebelled against the Spirit of God, and rash words came from Moses' lips. How much more severely do you think someone deserves to be punished who has insulted the Spirit of grace? These are the words of him who holds the seven spirits of God and the seven stars. I know your deeds; you have a reputation of being alive, but you are dead.

The Holy Spirit

If you love me, keep my commands. The Advocate, the Holy Spirit, whom the Father will send in my name, will teach you all things and will remind you of everything I have said to you. When the Advocate comes, whom I will send to you from the Father— the Spirit of truth who goes out from the Father—he will testify about me. And with that he breathed on them and said, Receive the Holy Spirit.
John baptized with water, but you will be baptized with the Holy Spirit.' God, who knows the heart, showed that he accepted them by giving the Holy Spirit to them, just as he did to us. When you believed, you were marked in him with a seal, the promised Holy Spirit. Anyone who rejects this instruction does not reject a human being but God, the very God who gives you his Holy Spirit. It is impossible for those who have once been enlightened, who have tasted the heavenly gift, who have shared in the Holy Spirit … God's love has

been poured out into our hearts through the Holy Spirit, who has been given to us. May the grace of the Lord Jesus Christ, and the love of God, and the fellowship of the Holy Spirit be with you all. Guard the good deposit that was entrusted to you—guard it with the help of the Holy Spirit who lives in us. For the kingdom of God is not a matter of eating and drinking, but of righteousness, peace and joy in the Holy Spirit. May the God of hope fill you with all joy and peace as you trust in him, so that you may overflow with hope by the power of the Holy Spirit. He saved us through the washing of rebirth and renewal by the Holy Spirit. Your bodies are temples of the Holy Spirit, who is in you, whom you have received from God? You are not your own.

Anyone who speaks against the Holy Spirit will not be forgiven, either in this age or in the age to come. Whoever blasphemes against the Holy Spirit will never be forgiven; they are guilty of an eternal sin. Go and make disciples of all nations, baptizing them in the name of the Father and of the Son and of the Holy Spirit.

Our Reflections:

Genesis 1:20-25

20 And God said, "Let the water teem with living creatures, and let birds fly above the earth across the vault of the sky." 21 So God created the great creatures of the sea and every living thing with which the water teems and that moves about in it, according to their kinds, and every winged bird according to its kind. And God saw that it was good. 22 God blessed them and said, "Be fruitful and increase in number and fill the water in the seas, and let the birds increase on the earth." 23 And there was evening, and there was morning—the fifth day. 24 And God said, "Let the land produce living creatures according to their kinds:the livestock, the creatures that move along the ground, and the wild animals, each according to its kind." And it was so. 25 God made the wild animals according to their kinds, the livestock according to their kinds, and all the creatures that move along the ground according to their kinds. And God saw that it was good.

Genesis 9:5-16

And for your lifeblood I will surely demand an **account**ing. I will demand an **account**ing from every animal. And from each human being, too, I will demand an **account**ing for the life of another human being. 8 Then God said to Noah and to his sons with him: 9 "I now establish my covenant with you and with your descendants after you 10 and with every living creature that was with you—the birds, the livestock and all the wild animals, all those that came out of the ark with you—every living creature on earth. 11 I establish my covenant with you: Never again will all life be destroyed by the waters of a flood; never again will there be a flood to destroy the earth." 12 And God said, "This is the sign of the covenant I am making between me and you and every living creature with you, a covenant for all generations to come: 13 I have set my rainbow in the clouds, and it will be the sign of the covenant between me and the earth. 14 Whenever I bring clouds over the earth and the rainbow appears in the clouds, 15 I will remember my covenant between me and you and all living creatures of every kind. Never again will the waters become a flood to destroy all life. 16 Whenever the rainbow appears in the clouds, I will see it and remember the everlasting covenant between God and all living creatures of every kind on the earth."

Leviticus 11:9
"'Of all the creatures **living** in the **water** of the seas and the streams you may eat any that have fins and scales.

Leviticus 11:46
"'These are the regulations concerning animals, birds, every **living** thing that moves about in the **water** and every creature that moves along the ground.

Jeremiah 2:13
"My people have committed two sins: They have forsaken me, the spring of **living water**, and have dug their own cisterns, broken cisterns that cannot hold **water**.

Jeremiah 17:13
Lord, you are the hope of Israel; all who forsake you will be put to shame. Those who turn away from you will be written in the dust because they have forsaken the Lord, the spring of **living water**.

Ezekiel 12:19
Say to the people of the land: 'This is what the Sovereign Lord says about those **living** in Jerusalem and in the land of Israel: They will eat their food in anxiety and drink their **water** in despair, for their land will be stripped of everything in it because of the violence of all who live there.

Ezekiel 47:9
Swarms of **living** creatures will live wherever the river flows. There will be large numbers of fish, because this **water** flows there and makes the salt **water** fresh; so where the river flows everything will live.

Zechariah 14:8
On that day **living water** will flow out from Jerusalem, half of it east to the Dead Sea and half of it west to the Mediterranean Sea, in summer and in winter.

John 4:10
Jesus answered her, "If you knew the gift of God and who it is that asks you for a drink, you would have asked him and he would have given you **living water**."

John 4:11
"Sir," the woman said, "you have nothing to draw with and the well is deep. Where can you get this **living water**?

John 7:38
Whoever believes in me, as Scripture has said, rivers of **living water** will flow from within them."

Revelation 7:17
For the Lamb at the center of the throne will be their shepherd; 'he will lead them to springs of **living water**.' 'And God will wipe away every tear from their eyes.'"

Job 12:7-12
Then Job replied:
"But ask the animals, and they will teach you,
　or the birds in the sky, and they will tell you;
or speak to the earth, and it will teach you,
　or let the fish in the sea inform you.
Which of all these does not know
　that the hand of the Lord has done this?
In his hand is the life of every creature
　and the breath of all mankind.
Does not the ear test words
　as the tongue tastes food?
Is not wisdom found among the aged?
　Does not long life bring understanding?

Genesis 2:7
7 Then the Lord God formed a man[a] from the dust of the ground and breathed into his nostrils the breath of life, and the man became a living being.

Genesis 1:21
21 So God created the great creatures of the sea and every living thing with which the water
　　teems and that moves about in it, according to their kinds, and every winged bird
　　according to its kind. And God saw that it was good.

Genesis 1:24
24 And God said, "Let the land produce living creatures according to their kinds: the livestock,
　　the creatures that move along the ground, and the wild animals, each according to its
　　kind." And it was so.

Isaiah 42:1
"Here is my servant, whom I uphold, my chosen one in whom I delight;
I will put my Spirit on him, and he will bring justice to the nations.

Jeremiah 6:8
8 Take warning, Jerusalem, or I will turn away from you
and make your land desolate so no one can live in it."

1 Samuel 18:1
After David had finished talking with Saul, Jonathan became one in spirit with David, and he loved him as himself.

Life-Soul, Body-Soul, as Living Water

The life- or body-soul is the run of the sturgeon, sucker and salmon up the fresh rivers and streams to begin the next generation and to be devoured by birds and bear, wolves and wolverines, mice and men. These bodies are immersed in the water that runs, that flows, that carries their vital life-force as a gift to other living beings. If that water is obstructed the life-force cannot continue to become the gifting it is. If the water stops, the life-force dies prematurely, again not reaching and continuing so the life-force may be transferred into other beings. If the water is tainted with toxins, the poisoned life-force silently kills those it would nourish. And, as the water flows onward, always downward, into the pond or lake or ocean it moves toward, it carries the obstructions, the stoppages, and the toxins with it, with the next generation of life-force running down, carried in return, to complete and continue what was once an ever-renewing circle of gifting. So the ponds, lakes and oceans become the memory, the retainer and reservoir, the accumulation of all that has promoted or destroyed the vitality of the life-force, the life-soul, the body-soul of all the inter-connected beings who partake of its living, life-giving essence. So it is with the soul of man; it is the reservoir of all the heart has chosen, that the mind and body have done.

If God sent the Spirit of his Son into my heart, writes upon my heart and pours his love into my heart, and if I call on the Lord to purify and cleanse my heart, to direct and guide my heart, there is a most critical question:

How am I to listen to, hear, see and understand what the Father, Son and Holy Spirit are pouring into my heart?

Some will say to read the Word (in Scripture) as the primary vehicle;
others will say to learn to read the actual feelings in my heart;
another will say to meditate and pray;
some may suggest to be open to messengers that come to me:
> through angels,
> through Creation (doves and donkeys),
> through dreams,
> through voices and visions.

Yet, why not learn to use all of these channels, tools, languages and voices? I realize that one problem, now, is that adults do not model, mentor and encourage such skills in children, and, rarely share such experiences with one another. Perhaps this has been our undoing, that we rarely gather together in small groups to share the gifts of the various messages from and of the Lord, that come variously, uniquely to each of us, so that we might gather them together in order that they might strengthen one another. Perhaps Leslie Silko says it best ...

Willow Twigs and Tangled Roots

For the people, it was that simple, and when they failed, the humiliation fell on all of them; what happened to the girl did not happen to her alone, it happened to all of them.

They focused the anger on the girl and her family, knowing from many years of this conflict that the anger could not be contained by a single person or family, but that it must leak out and soak into the ground under the entire village.

So Auntie had tried desperately to reconcile the family with the people; the old instinct had always been to gather the feelings and opinions that were scattered through the village, to gather them like willow twigs and tie them into a single prayer bundle that would bring peace to all of them. But now the feelings were twisted, tangled roots, and all the names for the source of this growth were buried under English words, out of reach. And there would be no peace and the people would have no rest until the entanglement had been unwound to the source.

(after Leslie Silko, 1977, in her Pulitzer winning book, *Ceremony*, p.69)

So I ask myself the crucial, expanded question:

How am I to listen to, hear, see and understand what the Lord is pouring into my heart, to be guided by such, and how am I to gather together with others and share what we have heard, seen and understood, the gifts of the Lord that have been poured into our hearts to make us one?

1 John 4 New International Version (NIV)

They are from the world and therefore speak from the viewpoint of the world, and the world listens to them. ⁶ We are from God, and whoever knows God listens to us; but whoever is not from God does not listen to us. This is how we recognize the Spirit[a] of truth and the spirit of falsehood.

⁷ Dear friends, let us love one another, for love comes from God. Everyone who loves has been born of God and knows God. ⁸ Whoever does not love does not know God, because God is love. ⁹ This is how God showed his love among us: He sent his one and only Son into the world that we might live through him. ¹⁰ This is love: not that we loved God, but that he loved us and sent his Son as an atoning sacrifice for our sins. ¹¹ Dear friends, since God so loved us, we also ought to love one another. ¹² No one has ever seen God; but if we love one another, God lives in us and his love is made complete in us.

¹³ This is how we know that we live in him and he in us: He has given us of his Spirit. ¹⁴ And we have seen and testify that the Father has sent his Son to be the Savior of the world. ¹⁵ If anyone acknowledges that Jesus is the Son of God, God lives in them and they in God. ¹⁶ And so we know and rely on the love God has for us.
God is love. Whoever lives in love lives in God, and God in them. ¹⁷ This is how love is made complete among us so that we will have confidence on the day of judgment: In this world we are like Jesus. ¹⁸ There is no fear in love. But perfect love drives out fear, because fear has to do with punishment. The one who fears is not made perfect in love.

¹⁹ We love because he first loved us. ²⁰ Whoever claims to love God yet hates a brother or sister is a liar. For whoever does not love their brother and sister, whom they have seen,cannot love God, whom they have not seen. ²¹ And he has given us this command: Anyone who loves God must also love their brother and sister.

Your Reflections:

Your Study Partner's Reflections:

Appendices

Heart in the New Testament (149 New Testament = 49 Gospels + 100 After)

<u>Heart in the Gospels</u> (49 = 21 positive + 28 negative)

Matthew 5:8
Blessed are the pure in **heart**, for they will see God.

Matthew 6:21
For where your treasure is, there your **heart** will be also.

Matthew 9:2
Some men brought to him a paralyzed man, lying on a mat. When Jesus saw their faith, he said to the man, "Take **heart**, son; your sins are forgiven."

Matthew 9:22
Jesus turned and saw her. "Take **heart**, daughter," he said, "your faith has healed you." And the woman was healed at that moment.

Matthew 11:29
Take my yoke upon you and learn from me, for I am gentle and humble in **heart**, and you will find rest for your souls.

Matthew 18:35
"This is how my heavenly Father will treat each of you unless you forgive your brother or sister from your **heart**."

Matthew 22:37
Jesus replied: "'Love the Lord your God with all your **heart** and with all your soul and with all your mind.'

Mark 11:23
"Truly I tell you, if anyone says to this mountain, 'Go, throw yourself into the sea,' and does not doubt in their **heart** but believes that what they say will happen, it will be done for them.

Mark 12:30
Love the Lord your God with all your **heart** and with all your soul and with all your mind and with all your strength.'

Mark 12:33
To love him with all your **heart**, with all your understanding and with all your strength, and to love your neighbor as yourself is more important than all burnt offerings and sacrifices."

Luke 2:19
But Mary treasured up all these things and pondered them in her **heart**.

Luke 2:51
Then he went down to Nazareth with them and was obedient to them. But his mother treasured all these things in her **heart**.

Luke 3:15
The people were waiting expectantly and were all wondering in their **heart**s if John might possibly be the Messiah.

Luke 8:15
But the seed on good soil stands for those with a noble and good **heart**, who hear the word, retain it, and by persevering produce a crop.

Luke 10:27
He answered, "'Love the Lord your God with all your **heart** and with all your soul and with all your strength and with all your mind'; and, 'Love your neighbor as yourself.'"

Luke 7:13
When the Lord saw her, his **heart** went out to her and he said, "Don't cry."

Luke 12:34
For where your treasure is, there your **heart** will be also.

Luke 24:32
They asked each other, "Were not our **heart**s burning within us while he talked with us on the road and opened the Scriptures to us?"

John 14:1
[*Jesus Comforts His Disciples*] "Do not let your **heart**s be troubled. You believe in God; believe also in me.

John 14:27
Peace I leave with you; my peace I give you. I do not give to you as the world gives. Do not let your **heart**s be troubled and do not be afraid.

John 16:33
"I have told you these things, so that in me you may have peace. In this world you will have trouble. But take **heart**! I have overcome the world."

Matthew 5:28
But I tell you that anyone who looks at a woman lustfully has already committed adultery with her in his **heart**.

Matthew 9:4
Knowing their thoughts, Jesus said, "Why do you entertain evil thoughts in your **heart**s?

Matthew 12:34
You brood of vipers, how can you who are evil say anything good? For the mouth speaks what the **heart** is full of.

Matthew 12:40
For as Jonah was three days and three nights in the belly of a huge fish, so the Son of Man will be three days and three nights in the **heart** of the earth.

Matthew 13:15
For this people's **heart** has become calloused; they hardly hear with their ears, and they have closed their eyes. Otherwise they might see with their eyes, hear with their ears, understand with their **heart**s and turn, and I would heal them.'

Matthew 13:19
When anyone hears the message about the kingdom and does not understand it, the evil one comes and snatches away what was sown in their **heart**. This is the seed sown along the path.

Matthew 15:8
"'These people honor me with their lips, but their **heart**s are far from me.

Matthew 15:18
But the things that come out of a person's mouth come from the **heart**, and these defile them.

Matthew 15:19
For out of the **heart** come evil thoughts—murder, adultery, sexual immorality, theft, false testimony, slander.

Matthew 19:8
Jesus replied, "Moses permitted you to divorce your wives because your **heart**s were hard. But it was not this way from the beginning.

Mark 2:8
Immediately Jesus knew in his spirit that this was what they were thinking in their **heart**s, and he said to them, "Why are you thinking these things?

Mark 3:5
He looked around at them in anger and, deeply distressed at their stubborn **heart**s, said to the man, "Stretch out your hand." He stretched it out, and his hand was completely restored.

Mark 6:52
for they had not understood about the loaves; their **heart**s were hardened.

Mark 7:6
He replied, "Isaiah was right when he prophesied about you hypocrites; as it is written: "'These people honor me with their lips, but their **heart**s are far from me.

Mark 7:19
For it doesn't go into their **heart** but into their stomach, and then out of the body." (In saying this, Jesus declared all foods clean.)

Mark 7:21
For it is from within, out of a person's **heart**, that evil thoughts come—sexual immorality, theft, murder,

Mark 8:17
Aware of their discussion, Jesus asked them: "Why are you talking about having no bread? Do you still not see or understand? Are your **heart**s hardened?

Mark 10:5
"It was because your **heart**s were hard that Moses wrote you this law," Jesus replied.

Luke 1:17
And he will go on before the Lord, in the spirit and power of Elijah, to turn the **heart**s of the parents to their children and the disobedient to the wisdom of the righteous—to make ready a people prepared for the Lord."

Luke 2:35
so that the thoughts of many **heart**s will be revealed. And a sword will pierce your own soul too."

Luke 5:22
Jesus knew what they were thinking and asked, "Why are you thinking these things in your **heart**s?

Luke 6:45
A good man brings good things out of the good stored up in his **heart**, and an evil man brings evil things out of the evil stored up in his **heart**. For the mouth speaks what the **heart** is full of.

Luke 8:12
Those along the path are the ones who hear, and then the devil comes and takes away the word from their **heart**s, so that they may not believe and be saved.

Luke 12:29
And do not set your **heart** on what you will eat or drink; do not worry about it.

Luke 16:15

He said to them, "You are the ones who justify yourselves in the eyes of others, but God knows your **heart**s. What people value highly is detestable in God's sight.

Luke 21:34

"Be careful, or your **heart**s will be weighed down with carousing, drunkenness and the anxieties of life, and that day will close on you suddenly like a trap.

John 5:42

but I know you. I know that you do not have the love of God in your **heart**s.

John 12:40

"He has blinded their eyes and hardened their **heart**s, so they can neither see with their eyes, nor understand with their **heart**s, nor turn—and I would heal them."

Heart in the New Testament after the Gospels (100 = 68 positive + 32 negative)

Acts 1:24
Then they prayed, "Lord, you know everyone's **heart**. Show us which of these two you have chosen

Acts 2:26
Therefore my **heart** is glad and my tongue rejoices; my body also will rest in hope,

Acts 2:46
Every day they continued to meet together in the temple courts. They broke bread in their homes and ate together with glad and sincere **heart**s,

Acts 4:32
[*The Believers Share Their Possessions*] All the believers were one in **heart** and mind. No one claimed that any of their possessions was their own, but they shared everything they had.

Acts 11:23
When he arrived and saw what the grace of God had done, he was glad and encouraged them all to remain true to the Lord with all their **heart**s.

Acts 13:22
After removing Saul, he made David their king. God testified concerning him: 'I have found David son of Jesse, a man after my own **heart**; he will do everything I want him to do.'

Acts 14:17
Yet he has not left himself without testimony: He has shown kindness by giving you rain from heaven and crops in their seasons; he provides you with plenty of food and fills your **heart**s with joy."

Acts 15:8
God, who knows the **heart**, showed that he accepted them by giving the Holy Spirit to them, just as he did to us.

Acts 15:9
He did not discriminate between us and them, for he purified their **heart**s by faith.

Acts 16:14
One of those listening was a woman from the city of Thyatira named Lydia, a dealer in purple cloth. She was a worshiper of God. The Lord opened her **heart** to respond to Paul's message.

Romans 2:15
They show that the requirements of the law are written on their **heart**s, their consciences also bearing witness, and their thoughts sometimes accusing them and at other times even defending them.)

Romans 2:29
No, a person is a Jew who is one inwardly; and circumcision is circumcision of the **heart**, by the Spirit, not by the written code. Such a person's praise is not from other people, but from God.

Romans 5:5
And hope does not put us to shame, because God's love has been poured out into our **heart**s through the Holy Spirit, who has been given to us.

Romans 6:17
But thanks be to God that, though you used to be slaves to sin, you have come to obey from your **heart** the pattern of teaching that has now claimed your allegiance.

Romans 8:27
And he who searches our **heart**s knows the mind of the Spirit, because the Spirit intercedes for God's people in accordance with the will of God.

Romans 10:1
Brothers and sisters, my **heart**'s desire and prayer to God for the Israelites is that they may be saved.

Romans 10:8
But what does it say? "The word is near you; it is in your mouth and in your **heart**," that is, the message concerning faith that we proclaim:

Romans 10:9
If you declare with your mouth, "Jesus is Lord," and believe in your **heart** that God raised him from the dead, you will be saved.

Romans 10:10
For it is with your **heart** that you believe and are justified, and it is with your mouth that you profess your faith and are saved.

1 Corinthians 4:5
Therefore judge nothing before the appointed time; wait until the Lord comes. He will bring to light what is hidden in darkness and will expose the motives of the **heart**. At that time each will receive their praise from God.

1 Corinthians 14:25
as the secrets of their **heart**s are laid bare. So they will fall down and worship God, exclaiming, "God is really among you!"

2 Corinthians 1:22
set his seal of ownership on us, and put his Spirit in our **heart**s as a deposit, guaranteeing what is to come.

2 Corinthians 3:2
You yourselves are our letter, written on our **heart**s, known and read by everyone.

2 Corinthians 3:3
You show that you are a letter from Christ, the result of our ministry, written not with ink but with the Spirit of the living God, not on tablets of stone but on tablets of human **heart**s.

2 Corinthians 4:1
[*Present Weakness and Resurrection Life*] Therefore, since through God's mercy we have this ministry, we do not lose **heart**.

2 Corinthians 4:6
For God, who said, "Let light shine out of darkness," made his light shine in our **heart**s to give us the light of the knowledge of God's glory displayed in the

2 Corinthians 4:16
Therefore we do not lose **heart**. Though outwardly we are wasting away, yet inwardly we are being renewed day by day.

2 Corinthians 6:11
We have spoken freely to you, Corinthians, and opened wide our **heart**s to you.

2 Corinthians 6:13
As a fair exchange—I speak as to my children—open wide your **heart**s also.

2 Corinthians 7:2
[*Paul's Joy Over the Church's Repentance*] Make room for us in your **heart**s. We have wronged no one, we have corrupted no one, we have exploited no one.

2 Corinthians 7:3
I do not say this to condemn you; I have said before that you have such a place in our **heart**s that we would live or die with you.

2 Corinthians 8:16
[*Titus Sent to Receive the Collection*] Thanks be to God, who put into the **heart** of Titus the same concern I have for you.

2 Corinthians 9:7
Each of you should give what you have decided in your **heart** to give, not reluctantly or under compulsion, for God loves a cheerful giver.

2 Corinthians 9:14
And in their prayers for you their cheerful to you, because of the surpassing grace God has given you.

Galatians 4:6
Because you are his sons, God sent the Spirit of his Son into our **heart**s, the Spirit who calls out, *"Abba*, Father."

Ephesians 1:18
I pray that the eyes of your **heart** may be enlightened in order that you may know the hope to which he has called you, the riches of his glorious inheritance in his holy people,

Ephesians 3:17
so that Christ may dwell in your **heart**s through faith. And I pray that you, being rooted and established in love,

Ephesians 5:19
speaking to one another with psalms, hymns, and songs from the Spirit. Sing and make music from your **heart** to the Lord,

Ephesians 6:5
Slaves, obey your earthly masters with respect and fear, and with sincerity of **heart**, just as you would obey Christ.

Ephesians 6:6
Obey them not only to win their favor when their eye is on you, but as slaves of Christ, doing the will of God from your **heart**.

Philippians 1:7
It is right for me to feel this way about all of you, since I have you in my **heart** and, whether I am in chains or defending and confirming the gospel, all of you share in God's grace with me.

Philippians 4:7
And the peace of God, which transcends all understanding, will guard your **heart**s and your minds in Christ Jesus.

Colossians 2:2
My goal is that they may be encouraged in **heart** and united in love, so that they may have the full riches of complete understanding, in order that they may know the mystery of God, namely, Christ,

Colossians 3:1
[*Living as Those Made Alive in Christ*] Since, then, you have been raised with Christ, set your **heart**s on things above, where Christ is, seated at the right hand of God.

Colossians 3:15
Let the peace of Christ rule in your **heart**s, since as members of one body you were called to peace. And be thankful.

Colossians 3:16
Let the message of Christ dwell among you richly as you teach and admonish one another with all wisdom through psalms, hymns, and songs from the Spirit, singing to God with gratitude in your **heart**s.

Colossians 3:22
Slaves, obey your earthly masters in everything; and do it, not only when their eye is on you and to curry their favor, but with sincerity of **heart** and reverence for the Lord.

Colossians 3:23
Whatever you do, work at it with all your **heart**, as working for the Lord, not for human masters,

Colossians 4:8
I am sending him to you for the express purpose that you may know about our circumstances and that he may encourage your **heart**s.

1 Thessalonians 3:13
May he strengthen your **heart**s so that you will be blameless and holy in the presence of our God and Father when our Lord Jesus comes with all his holy ones.

2 Thessalonians 2:17
encourage your **heart**s and strengthen you in every good deed and word.

2 Thessalonians 3:5
May the Lord direct your **heart**s into God's love and Christ's perseverance.

1 Timothy 1:5
The goal of this command is love, which comes from a pure **heart** and a good conscience and a sincere faith.

2 Timothy 2:22
Flee the evil desires of youth and pursue righteousness, faith, love and peace, along with those who call on the Lord out of a pure **heart**.

Philemon 1:7
Your love has given me great joy and encouragement, because you, brother, have refreshed the **heart**s of the Lord's people.

Philemon 1:12
I am sending him—who is my very **heart**—back to you.

Philemon 1:20
I do wish, brother, that I may have some benefit from you in the Lord; refresh my **heart** in Christ.

Hebrews 8:10
This is the covenant I will establish with the people of Israel after that time, declares the Lord. I will put my laws in their minds and write them on their **heart**s. I will be their God, and they will be my people.

Hebrews 10:16
"This is the covenant I will make with them after that time, says the Lord. I will put my laws in their **heart**s, and I will write them on their minds."

Hebrews 10:22
let us draw near to God with a sincere **heart** and with the full assurance that faith brings, having our **heart**s sprinkled to cleanse us from a guilty conscience and having our bodies washed with pure water.

Hebrews 13:9
Do not be carried away by all kinds of strange teachings. It is good for our **heart**s to be strengthened by grace, not by eating ceremonial foods, which is of no benefit to those who do so.

James 4:8
Come near to God and he will come near to you. Wash your hands, you sinners, and purify your **heart**s, you double-minded.

1 Peter 1:22
Now that you have purified yourselves by obeying the truth so that you have sincere love for each other, love one another deeply, from the **heart**.

1 Peter 3:15
But in your **heart**s revere Christ as Lord. Always be prepared to give an answer to everyone who asks you to give the reason for the hope that you have. But do this with gentleness and respect,

2 Peter 1:19
We also have the prophetic message as something completely reliable, and you will do well to pay attention to it, as to a light shining in a dark place, until the day dawns and the morning star rises in your **heart**s.

1 John 3:19
This is how we know that we belong to the truth and how we set our **heart**s at rest in his presence:

Revelation 1:3
Blessed is the one who reads aloud the words of this prophecy, and blessed are those who hear it and take to **heart** what is written in it, because the time is near.

Revelation 17:17
For God has put it into their **heart**s to accomplish his purpose by agreeing to hand over to the beast their royal authority, until God's words are fulfilled.

Acts 2:37
When the people heard this, they were cut to the **heart** and said to Peter and the other apostles, "Brothers, what shall we do?"

Acts 5:3
Then Peter said, "Ananias, how is it that Satan has so filled your **heart** that you have lied to the Holy Spirit and have kept for yourself some of the money you received for the land?

Acts 7:39
"But our ancestors refused to obey him. Instead, they rejected him and in their **heart**s turned back to Egypt.

Acts 7:51
"You stiff-necked people! Your **heart**s and ears are still uncircumcised. You are just like your ancestors: You always resist the Holy Spirit!

Acts 8:21
You have no part or share in this ministry, because your **heart** is not right before God.

Acts 8:22
Repent of this wickedness and pray to the Lord in the hope that he may forgive you for having such a thought in your **heart**.

Acts 21:13
Then Paul answered, "Why are you weeping and breaking my **heart**? I am ready not only to be bound, but also to die in Jerusalem for the name of the Lord Jesus."

Acts 28:27
For this people's **heart** has become calloused; they hardly hear with their ears, and they have closed their eyes. Otherwise they might see with their eyes, hear with their ears, understand with their **heart**s and turn, and I would heal them.'

Romans 1:21
For although they knew God, they neither glorified him as God nor gave thanks to him, but their thinking became futile and their foolish **heart**s were darkened.

Romans 1:24
Therefore God gave them over in the sinful desires of their **heart**s to sexual impurity for the degrading of their bodies with one another.

Romans 2:5
But because of your stubbornness and your unrepentant **heart**, you are storing up wrath against yourself for the day of God's wrath, when his righteous judgment will be revealed.

Romans 9:2
I have great sorrow and unceasing anguish in my **heart**.

Romans 10:6
But the righteousness that is by faith says: "Do not say in your **heart**, 'Who will ascend into heaven?'" (that is, to bring Christ down)

1 Corinthians 10:6
Now these things occurred as examples to keep us from setting our **heart**s on evil things as they did.

2 Corinthians 2:4
For I wrote you out of great distress and anguish of **heart** and with many tears, not to grieve you but to let you know the depth of my love for you.

2 Corinthians 3:15
Even to this day when Moses is read, a veil covers their **heart**s.

2 Corinthians 5:12
We are not trying to commend ourselves to you again, but are giving you an opportunity to take pride in us, so that you can answer those who take pride in what is seen rather than in what is in the **heart**.

Ephesians 4:18
They are darkened in their understanding and separated from the life of God because of the ignorance that is in them due to the hardening of their **heart**s.

1 Thessalonians 2:4
On the contrary, we speak as those approved by God to be entrusted with the gospel. We are not trying to please people but God, who tests our **heart**s.

Hebrews 3:8
do not harden your **heart**s as you did in the rebellion, during the time of testing in the wilderness,

Hebrews 3:10
That is why I was angry with that generation; I said, 'Their **heart**s are always going astray, and they have not known my ways.'

Hebrews 3:12
See to it, brothers and sisters, that none of you has a sinful, unbelieving **heart** that turns away from the living God.

Hebrews 3:15
As has just been said: "Today, if you hear his voice, do not harden your **heart**s as you did in the rebellion."

Hebrews 4:7
God again set a certain day, calling it "Today." This he did when a long time later he spoke through David, as in the passage already quoted: "Today, if you hear his voice, do not harden your **heart**s."

Hebrews 4:12
For the word of God is alive and active. Sharper than any double-edged sword, it penetrates even to dividing soul and spirit, joints and marrow; it judges the thoughts and attitudes of the **heart**.

Hebrews 12:3
Consider him who endured such opposition from sinners, so that you will not grow weary and lose **heart**.

Hebrews 12:5
And have you completely forgotten this word of encouragement that addresses you as a father addresses his son? It says, "My son, do not make light of the Lord's discipline, and do not lose **heart** when he rebukes you,

James 3:14
But if you harbor bitter envy and selfish ambition in your **heart**s, do not boast about it or deny the truth.

1 John 3:20
If our **heart**s condemn us, we know that God is greater than our **heart**s, and he knows everything.

1 John 3:21
Dear friends, if our **heart**s do not condemn us, we have confidence before God

Revelation 2:23
I will strike her children dead. Then all the churches will know that I am he who searches **heart**s and minds, and I will repay each of you according to your deeds.

Revelation 18:7
Give her as much torment and grief as the glory and luxury she gave herself. In her **heart** she boasts, 'I sit enthroned as queen. I am not a widow; I will never mourn.'

Soul　(95 Total = 72 OT + 23 NT)
　　　　[58 passages, soul only = 26 Negative + 32 Positive]

Job 3:20
"Why is light given to those in misery, and life to the bitter of **soul**,

Job 10:1
"I loathe my very life; therefore I will give free rein to my complaint and speak out in the bitterness of my **soul**.

Job 21:25
Another dies in bitterness of **soul**, never having enjoyed anything good.

Job 24:12
The groans of the dying rise from the city, and the **soul**s of the wounded cry out for help. But God charges no one with wrongdoing.

Job 30:25
Have I not wept for those in trouble? Has not my **soul** grieved for the poor?

Psalm 6:3
My **soul** is in deep anguish. How long, Lord, how long?

Psalm 26:9
Do not take away my **soul** along with sinners, my life with those who are bloodthirsty,

Psalm 31:7
I will be glad and rejoice in your love, for you saw my affliction and knew the anguish of my **soul**.

Psalm 42:5
Why, my **soul**, are you downcast? Why so disturbed within me? Put your hope in God, for I will yet praise him, my Savior and my God.

Psalm 42:6
My **soul** is downcast within me; therefore I will remember you from the land of the Jordan, the heights of Hermon—from Mount Mizar.

Psalm 42:11
Why, my **soul**, are you downcast? Why so disturbed within me?

Psalm 43:5
Why, my **soul**, are you downcast? Why so disturbed within me? Put your hope in God, for I will yet praise him, my Savior and my God.

Psalm 119:28
My **soul** is weary with sorrow; strengthen me according to your word.

Proverbs 1:11-12
If they say, "Come along with us; let's lie in wait for innocent blood, let's ambush some harmless **soul**; let's swallow them alive, like the grave, and whole, like those who go down to the pit;

Isaiah 38:15
But what can I say? He has spoken to me, and he himself has done this. I will walk humbly all my years because of this anguish of my **soul**.

Lamentations 3:20
I well remember them, and my **soul** is downcast within me.

Lamentations 3:51
What I see brings grief to my **soul** because of all the women of my city.

Ezekiel 27:31
They will shave their heads because of you and will put on sackcloth. They will weep over you with anguish of **soul** and with bitter mourning.

Matthew 16:26
What good will it be for someone to gain the whole world, yet forfeit their **soul**? Or what can anyone give in exchange for their **soul**?

Mark 8:36
What good is it for someone to gain the whole world, yet forfeit their **soul**?

Mark 8:37
Or what can anyone give in exchange for their **soul**?

Matthew 26:38
Then he said to them, "My **soul** is overwhelmed with sorrow to the point of death. Stay here and keep watch with me."

Mark 14:34
"My **soul** is overwhelmed with sorrow to the point of death," he said to them. "Stay here and keep watch."

John 12:27
"Now my **soul** is troubled, and what shall I say? 'Father, save me from this hour'? No, it was for this very reason I came to this hour.

1 Peter 2:11
[*Living Godly Lives in a Pagan Society*] Dear friends, I urge you, as foreigners and exiles, to abstain from sinful desires, which wage war against your **soul**.

2 Peter 2:8
(for that righteous man, living among them day after day, was tormented in his righteous **soul** by the lawless deeds he saw and heard)—

32 Positive

Judges 5:21
The river Kishon swept them away, the age-old river, the river Kishon. March on, my **soul**; be strong!

1 Samuel 1:15
"Not so, my lord," Hannah replied, "I am a woman who is deeply troubled. I have not been drinking wine or beer; I was pouring out my **soul** to the Lord.

Psalm 19:7
The law of the Lord is perfect, refreshing the **soul**. The statutes of the Lord are trustworthy, making wise the simple.

Psalm 23:3
he refreshes my **soul**. He guides me along the right paths for his name's sake.

Psalm 35:9
Then my **soul** will rejoice in the Lord and delight in his salvation.

Psalm 42:1
[*BOOK II*] [*Psalms 42–72*] [*Psalm 42*] [*For the director of music. A maskil of the Sons of Korah.*] As the deer pants for streams of water, so my **soul** pants for you, my God.

Psalm 42:2
My **soul** thirsts for God, for the living God. When can I go and meet with God?

Psalm 42:4
These things I remember as I pour out my **soul**: how I used to go to the house of God under the protection of the Mighty One with shouts of joy and praise among the festive throng.

Psalm 57:8
Awake, my **soul**! Awake, harp and lyre! I will awaken the dawn.

Psalm 62:1
[*Psalm 62*] [*For the director of music. For Jeduthun. A psalm of David.*] Truly my **soul** finds rest in God; my salvation comes from him.

Psalm 62:5
Yes, my **soul**, find rest in God; my hope comes from him.

Psalm 103:1
[*Psalm 103*] [*Of David.*] Praise the Lord, my **soul**; all my inmost being, praise his holy name.

Psalm 103:2
Praise the Lord, my **soul**, and forget not all his benefits—

Psalm 103:22
Praise the Lord, all his works everywhere in his dominion. Praise the Lord, my **soul**.

Psalm 104:1
[*Psalm 104*] Praise the Lord, my **soul**. Lord my God, you are very great; you are clothed with splendor and majesty.

Psalm 104:35
But may sinners vanish from the earth and the wicked be no more. Praise the Lord, my **soul**. Praise the Lord.

Psalm 116:7
Return to your rest, my **soul**, for the Lord has been good to you.

Psalm 119:20
My **soul** is consumed with longing for your laws at all times.

Psalm 119:81
[*כ Kaph*] My **soul** faints with longing for your salvation, but I have put my hope in your word.

Psalm 146:1
[*Psalm 146*] Praise the Lord. Praise the Lord, my **soul**.

Proverbs 13:19
A longing fulfilled is sweet to the **soul**, but fools detest turning from evil.

Proverbs 25:25
Like cold water to a weary **soul** is good news from a distant land.

Isaiah 61:10
I delight greatly in the Lord; my **soul** rejoices in my God. For he has clothed me with garments of salvation and arrayed me in a robe of his righteousness, as a bridegroom adorns his head like a priest, and as a bride adorns herself with her jewels.

Jeremiah 6:16
This is what the Lord says: "Stand at the crossroads and look; ask for the ancient paths, ask where the good way is, and walk in it, and you will find rest for your **soul**s. But you said, 'We will not walk in it.'

Matthew 11:29
Take my yoke upon you and learn from me, for I am gentle and humble in heart, and you will find rest for your **soul**s.

Luke 1:46
[*Mary's Song*] And Mary said: "My **soul** glorifies the Lord

Hebrews 6:19
We have this hope as an anchor for the **soul**, firm and secure. It enters the inner sanctuary behind the curtain,

1 Peter 1:9
for you are receiving the end result of your faith, the salvation of your **soul**s.

1 Peter 2:25
For "you were like sheep going astray," but now you have returned to the Shepherd and Overseer of your **soul**s.

3 John 1:2
Dear friend, I pray that you may enjoy good health and that all may go well with you, even as your **soul** is getting along well.

Revelation 6:9
When he opened the fifth seal, I saw under the altar the **soul**s of those who had been slain because of the word of God and the testimony they had maintained.

Revelation 20:4
I saw thrones on which were seated those who had been given authority to judge. And I saw the **soul**s of those who had been beheaded because of their testimony about Jesus and because of the word of God. They had not worshiped the beast or its image and had not received its mark on their foreheads or their hands. They came to life and reigned with Christ a thousand years.

<u>Spirit</u> (270 passages New Testament = 100 Gospels + 170)

Gospels (100 passages = 11 spirit + 30 impure spirit + 54 Holy Spirit)

<u>Spirit</u> <u>(11 passages)</u>

Matthew 5:3
"Blessed are the poor in **spirit**, for theirs is the kingdom of heaven.

Matthew 26:41
"Watch and pray so that you will not fall into temptation. The **spirit** is willing, but the flesh is weak."

Matthew 27:50
And when Jesus had cried out again in a loud voice, he gave up his **spirit**.

Mark 2:8
Immediately Jesus knew in his **spirit** that this was what they were thinking in their hearts, and he said to them, "Why are you thinking these things?

Mark 14:38
Watch and pray so that you will not fall into temptation. The **spirit** is willing, but the flesh is weak."

Luke 1:17
And he will go on before the Lord, in the **spirit** and power of Elijah, to turn the hearts of the parents to their children and the disobedient to the wisdom of the righteous—to make ready a people prepared for the Lord."

Luke 1:80
And the child grew and became strong in **spirit**; and he lived in the wilderness until he appeared publicly to Israel.

Luke 8:55
Her **spirit** returned, and at once she stood up. Then Jesus told them to give her something to eat.

Luke 23:46
Jesus called out with a loud voice, "Father, into your hands I commit my **spirit**." When he had said this, he breathed his last.

John 11:33
When Jesus saw her weeping, and the Jews who had come along with her also weeping, he was deeply moved in **spirit** and troubled.

John 13:21
After he had said this, Jesus was troubled in **spirit** and testified, "Very truly I tell you, one of you is going to betray me."

Impure Spirits (35 passages)

Matthew 8:16
When evening came, many who were demon-possessed were brought to him, and he drove out the **spirit**s with a word and healed all the sick.

Matthew 10:1
[*Jesus Sends Out the Twelve*] Jesus called his twelve disciples to him and gave them authority to drive out impure **spirit**s and to heal every disease and sickness.

Matthew 12:43
"When an impure **spirit** comes out of a person, it goes through arid places seeking rest and does not find it.

Matthew 12:45
Then it goes and takes with it seven other **spirit**s more wicked than itself, and they go in and live there. And the final condition of that person is worse than the first. That is how it will be with this wicked generation."

Mark 1:21
[*Jesus Drives Out an Impure **Spirit***] They went to Capernaum, and when the Sabbath came, Jesus went into the synagogue and began to teach.

Mark 1:23
Just then a man in their synagogue who was possessed by an impure **spirit** cried out,

Mark 1:26
The impure **spirit** shook the man violently and came out of him with a shriek.

Mark 1:27
The people were all so amazed that they asked each other, "What is this? A new teaching—and with authority! He even gives orders to impure **spirit**s and they obey him."

Mark 3:11
Whenever the impure **spirit**s saw him, they fell down before him and cried out, "You are the Son of God."

Mark 3:30
He said this because they were saying, "He has an impure **spirit**."

Mark 5:2
When Jesus got out of the boat, a man with an impure **spirit** came from the tombs to meet him.

Mark 5:8
For Jesus had said to him, "Come out of this man, you impure **spirit**!"

Mark 5:13
He gave them permission, and the impure **spirit**s came out and went into the pigs. The herd, about two thousand in number, rushed down the steep bank into the lake and were drowned.

Mark 6:7
Calling the Twelve to him, he began to send them out two by two and gave them authority over impure **spirit**s.

Mark 7:25
In fact, as soon as she heard about him, a woman whose little daughter was possessed by an impure **spirit** came and fell at his feet.

Mark 9:14
[*Jesus Heals a Boy Possessed by an Impure **Spirit***] When they came to the other disciples, they saw a large crowd around them and the teachers of the law arguing with them.

Mark 9:17
A man in the crowd answered, "Teacher, I brought you my son, who is possessed by a **spirit** that has robbed him of speech.

Mark 9:18
Whenever it seizes him, it throws him to the ground. He foams at the mouth, gnashes his teeth and becomes rigid. I asked your disciples to drive out the **spirit**, but they could not."

Mark 9:20
So they brought him. When the **spirit** saw Jesus, it immediately threw the boy into a convulsion. He fell to the ground and rolled around, foaming at the mouth.

Mark 9:25
When Jesus saw that a crowd was running to the scene, he rebuked the impure **spirit**. "You deaf and mute **spirit**," he said, "I command you, come out of him and never enter him again."

Mark 9:26
The **spirit** shrieked, convulsed him violently and came out. The boy looked so much like a corpse that many said, "He's dead."

Luke 4:31
[*Jesus Drives Out an Impure Spirit*] Then he went down to Capernaum, a town in Galilee, and on the Sabbath he taught the people.

Luke 4:33
In the synagogue there was a man possessed by a demon, an impure **spirit**. He cried out at the top of his voice,

Luke 4:36
All the people were amazed and said to each other, "What words these are! With authority and power he gives orders to impure **spirits** and they come out!"

Luke 6:18
who had come to hear him and to be healed of their diseases. Those troubled by impure **spirits** were cured,

Luke 7:21
At that very time Jesus cured many who had diseases, sicknesses and evil **spirits**, and gave sight to many who were blind.

Luke 8:2
and also some women who had been cured of evil **spirits** and diseases: Mary (called Magdalene) from whom seven demons had come out;

Luke 8:29
For Jesus had commanded the impure **spirit** to come out of the man. Many times it had seized him, and though he was chained hand and foot and kept under guard, he had broken his chains and had been driven by the demon into solitary places.

Luke 9:39
A **spirit** seizes him and he suddenly screams; it throws him into convulsions so that he foams at the mouth. It scarcely ever leaves him and is destroying him.

Luke 9:42
Even while the boy was coming, the demon threw him to the ground in a convulsion. But Jesus rebuked the impure **spirit**, healed the boy and gave him back to his father.

Luke 10:20
However, do not rejoice that the **spirits** submit to you, but rejoice that your names are written in heaven."

Luke 11:24
"When an impure **spirit** comes out of a person, it goes through arid places seeking rest and does not find it. Then it says, 'I will return to the house I left.'

Luke 11:26
Then it goes and takes seven other **spirit**s more wicked than itself, and they go in and live there. And the final condition of that person is worse than the first.

Luke 13:11
and a woman was there who had been crippled by a **spirit** for eighteen years. She was bent over and could not straighten up at all.

<u>Spirit</u> (270 passages New Testament = 100 Gospels + 170)

After Gospels (170 passages = 52 spirit + 18 impure spirit + 100 Holy Spirit)

<u>Spirit (52 passages)</u>

Acts 7:59
While they were stoning him, Stephen prayed, "Lord Jesus, receive my **spirit**."

Acts 23:8
(The Sadducees say that there is no resurrection, and that there are neither angels nor **spirit**s, but the Pharisees believe all these things.)

Acts 23:9
There was a great uproar, and some of the teachers of the law who were Pharisees stood up and argued vigorously. "We find nothing wrong with this man," they said. "What if a **spirit** or an angel has spoken to him?"

Romans 11:8
as it is written: "God gave them a **spirit** of stupor, eyes that could not see and ears that could not hear, to this very day."

Romans 1:9
God, whom I serve in my **spirit** in preaching the gospel of his Son, is my witness how constantly I remember you

Romans 1:11
I long to see you so that I may impart to you some **spirit**ual gift to make you strong—

Romans 12:11
Never be lacking in zeal, but keep your **spirit**ual fervor, serving the Lord.

Romans 15:27
They were pleased to do it, and indeed they owe it to them. For if the Gentiles have shared in the Jews' **spirit**ual blessings, they owe it to the Jews to share with them their material blessings.

1 Corinthians 1:7
Therefore you do not lack any **spirit**ual gift as you eagerly wait for our Lord Jesus Christ to be revealed.

1 Corinthians 4:21
What do you prefer? Shall I come to you with a rod of discipline, or shall I come in love and with a gentle **spirit**?

1 Corinthians 5:3
For my part, even though I am not physically present, I am with you in **spirit**. As one who is present with you in this way, I have already passed judgment in the name of our Lord Jesus on the one who has been doing this.

1 Corinthians 5:4
So when you are assembled and I am with you in **spirit**, and the power of our Lord Jesus is present,

1 Corinthians 5:5
hand this man over to Satan for the destruction of the flesh, so that his **spirit** may be saved on the day of the Lord.

1 Corinthians 6:17
But whoever is united with the Lord is one with him in **spirit**.

1 Corinthians 7:34
and his interests are divided. An unmarried woman or virgin is concerned about the Lord's affairs: Her aim is to be devoted to the Lord in both body and **spirit**. But a married woman is concerned about the affairs of this world—how she can please her husband.

1 Corinthians 9:11
If we have sown **spirit**ual seed among you, is it too much if we reap a material harvest from you?

1 Corinthians 10:3
They all ate the same **spirit**ual food

1 Corinthians 10:4
and drank the same **spirit**ual drink; for they drank from the **spirit**ual rock that accompanied them, and that rock was Christ.

1 Corinthians 12:10
to another miraculous powers, to another prophecy, to another distinguishing between **spirit**s, to another speaking in different kinds of tongues, and to still another the interpretation of tongues.

1 Corinthians 14:14
For if I pray in a tongue, my **spirit** prays, but my mind is unfruitful.

1 Corinthians 14:15
So what shall I do? I will pray with my **spirit**, but I will also pray with my understanding; I will sing with my **spirit**, but I will also sing with my understanding.

1 Corinthians 14:32
The **spirit**s of prophets are subject to the control of prophets.

1 Corinthians 15:44
it is sown a natural body, it is raised a **spirit**ual body. If there is a natural body, there is also a **spirit**ual body.

1 Corinthians 15:45
So it is written: "The first man Adam became a living being"; the last Adam, a life-giving **spirit**.

1 Corinthians 15:46
The **spirit**ual did not come first, but the natural, and after that the **spirit**ual.

1 Corinthians 16:18
For they refreshed my **spirit** and yours also. Such men deserve recognition.

2 Corinthians 4:13
It is written: "I believed; therefore I have spoken." Since we have that same **spirit** of faith, we also believe and therefore speak,

2 Corinthians 7:1
Therefore, since we have these promises, dear friends, let us purify ourselves from everything that contaminates body and **spirit**, perfecting holiness out of reverence for God.

2 Corinthians 7:13
By all this we are encouraged. In addition to our own encouragement, we were especially delighted to see how happy Titus was, because his **spirit** has been refreshed by all of you.

Galatians 6:18
The grace of our Lord Jesus Christ be with your **spirit**, brothers and sisters. Amen.

Ephesians 1:3
[*Praise for **Spirit**ual Blessings in Christ*] Praise be to the God and Father of our Lord Jesus Christ, who has blessed us in the heavenly realms with every **spirit**ual blessing in Christ.

Philippians 2:2
then make my joy complete by being like-minded, having the same love, being one in **spirit** and of one mind.

Philippians 4:23
The grace of the Lord Jesus Christ be with your **spirit**. Amen.

Colossians 2:5
For though I am absent from you in body, I am present with you in **spirit** and delight to see how disciplined you are and how firm your faith in Christ is.

1 Thessalonians 5:23
May God himself, the God of peace, sanctify you through and through. May your whole **spirit**, soul and body be kept blameless at the coming of our Lord Jesus Christ.

Philemon 1:25
The grace of the Lord Jesus Christ be with your **spirit**.

Hebrews 1:7
In speaking of the angels he says, "He makes his angels **spirit**s, and his servants flames of fire."

Hebrews 1:14
Are not all angels ministering **spirit**s sent to serve those who will inherit salvation?

Hebrews 4:12
For the word of God is alive and active. Sharper than any double-edged sword, it penetrates even to dividing soul and **spirit**, joints and marrow; it judges the thoughts and attitudes of the heart.

Hebrews 12:9
Moreover, we have all had human fathers who disciplined us and we respected them for it. How much more should we submit to the Father of **spirit**s and live!

Hebrews 12:23
to the church of the firstborn, whose names are written in heaven. You have come to God, the Judge of all, to the **spirit**s of the righteous made perfect,

James 2:26
As the body without the **spirit** is dead, so faith without deeds is dead.

James 4:5
Or do you think Scripture says without reason that he jealously longs for the **spirit** he has caused to dwell in us?

2 Timothy 4:22
The Lord be with your **spirit**. Grace be with you all.

1 Peter 2:2
Like newborn babies, crave pure **spirit**ual milk, so that by it you may grow up in your salvation,

1 Peter 2:5
you also, like living stones, are being built into a **spirit**ual house to be a holy priesthood, offering **spirit**ual sacrifices acceptable to God through Jesus Christ.

1 Peter 3:4
Rather, it should be that of your inner self, the unfading beauty of a gentle and quiet **spirit**, which is of great worth in God's sight.

1 Peter 3:19
After being made alive, he went and made proclamation to the imprisoned **spirit**s—

1 Peter 4:6
For this is the reason the gospel was preached even to those who are now dead, so that they might be judged according to human standards in regard to the body, but live according to God in regard to the **spirit**.

Revelation 1:4
[*Greetings and Doxology*] John, To the seven churches in the province of Asia: Grace and peace to you from him who is, and who was, and who is to come, and from the seven **spirit**s before his throne,

Revelation 4:5
From the throne came flashes of lightning, rumblings and peals of thunder. In front of the throne, seven lamps were blazing. These are the seven **spirit**s of God.

Revelation 5:6
Then I saw a Lamb, looking as if it had been slain, standing at the center of the throne, encircled by the four living creatures and the elders. The Lamb had seven horns and seven eyes, which are the seven **spirit**s of God sent out into all the earth.

Impure Spirit (18 passages)

Acts 5:16
Crowds gathered also from the towns around Jerusalem, bringing their sick and those tormented by impure **spirit**s, and all of them were healed.

Acts 8:7
For with shrieks, impure **spirit**s came out of many, and many who were paralyzed or lame were healed.

Acts 16:16
[*Paul and Silas in Prison*] Once when we were going to the place of prayer, we were met by a female slave who had a **spirit** by which she predicted the future. She earned a great deal of money for her owners by fortune-telling.

Acts 16:18
She kept this up for many days. Finally Paul became so annoyed that he turned around and said to the **spirit**, "In the name of Jesus Christ I command you to come out of her!" At that moment the **spirit** left her.

Acts 19:12
so that even handkerchiefs and aprons that had touched him were taken to the sick, and their illnesses were cured and the evil **spirit**s left them.

Acts 19:13
Some Jews who went around driving out evil **spirit**s tried to invoke the name of the Lord Jesus over those who were demon-possessed. They would say, "In the name of the Jesus whom Paul preaches, I command you to come out."

Acts 19:15
One day the evil **spirit** answered them, "Jesus I know, and Paul I know about, but who are you?"

Acts 19:16
Then the man who had the evil **spirit** jumped on them and overpowered them all. He gave them such a beating that they ran out of the house naked and bleeding.

Galatians 4:3
So also, when we were underage, we were in slavery under the elemental **spirit**ual forces of the world.

Ephesians 2:2
in which you used to live when you followed the ways of this world and of the ruler of the kingdom of the air, the **spirit** who is now at work in those who are disobedient.

Ephesians 6:12
For our struggle is not against flesh and blood, but against the rulers, against the authorities, against the powers of this dark world and against the **spirit**ual forces of evil in the heavenly realms.

Colossians 2:8
See to it that no one takes you captive through hollow and deceptive philosophy, which depends on human tradition and the elemental **spirit**ual forces of this world rather than on Christ.

Colossians 2:20
Since you died with Christ to the elemental **spirit**ual forces of this world, why, as though you still belonged to the world, do you submit to its rules:

1 Timothy 4:1
The **Spirit** clearly says that in later times some will abandon the faith and follow deceiving **spirit**s and things taught by demons.

1 John 4:1
[*On Denying the Incarnation*] Dear friends, do not believe every **spirit**, but test the **spirit**s to see whether they are from God, because many false prophets have gone out into the world.

1 John 4:3
but every **spirit** that does not acknowledge Jesus is not from God. This is the **spirit** of the antichrist, which you have heard is coming and even now is already in the world.

Revelation 16:13
Then I saw three impure **spirit**s that looked like frogs; they came out of the mouth of the dragon, out of the mouth of the beast and out of the mouth of the false prophet.

Revelation 16:14
They are demonic **spirit**s that perform signs, and they go out to the kings of the whole world, to gather them for the battle on the great day of God Almighty.

Demons in NT (76 passages)

Matthew 4:24
News about him spread all over Syria, and people brought to him all who were ill with various diseases, those suffering severe pain, the **demon**-possessed, those having seizures, and the paralyzed; and he healed them.

Matthew 7:22
Many will say to me on that day, 'Lord, Lord, did we not prophesy in your name and in your name drive out **demon**s and in your name perform many miracles?'

Matthew 8:16
When evening came, many who were **demon**-possessed were brought to him, and he drove out the spirits with a word and healed all the sick.

Matthew 8:28
[*Jesus Restores Two **Demon**-Possessed Men*] When he arrived at the other side in the region of the Gadarenes, two **demon**-possessed men coming from the tombs met him. They were so violent that no one could pass that way.

Matthew 8:31
The **demon**s begged Jesus, "If you drive us out, send us into the herd of pigs."

Matthew 8:33
Those tending the pigs ran off, went into the town and reported all this, including what had happened to the **demon**-possessed men.

Matthew 9:32
While they were going out, a man who was **demon**-possessed and could not talk was brought to Jesus.

Matthew 9:33
And when the **demon** was driven out, the man who had been mute spoke. The crowd was amazed and said, "Nothing like this has ever been seen in Israel."

Matthew 9:34
But the Pharisees said, "It is by the prince of **demon**s that he drives out **demon**s."

Matthew 10:8
Heal the sick, raise the dead, cleanse those who have leprosy, drive out **demon**s. Freely you have received; freely give.

Matthew 11:18
For John came neither eating nor drinking, and they say, 'He has a **demon**.'

Matthew 12:22
[*Jesus and Beelzebul*] Then they brought him a **demon**-possessed man who was blind and mute, and Jesus healed him, so that he could both talk and see.

Matthew 12:24
But when the Pharisees heard this, they said, "It is only by Beelzebul, the prince of **demon**s, that this fellow drives out **demon**s."

Matthew 12:27
And if I drive out **demon**s by Beelzebul, by whom do your people drive them out? So then, they will be your judges.

Matthew 12:28
But if it is by the Spirit of God that I drive out **demon**s, then the kingdom of God has come upon you.

Matthew 15:22
A Canaanite woman from that vicinity came to him, crying out, "Lord, Son of David, have mercy on me! My daughter is **demon**-possessed and suffering terribly."

Matthew 17:14
[*Jesus Heals a **Demon**-Possessed Boy*] When they came to the crowd, a man approached Jesus and knelt before him.

Matthew 17:18
Jesus rebuked the **demon**, and it came out of the boy, and he was healed at that moment.

Mark 1:32
That evening after sunset the people brought to Jesus all the sick and **demon**-possessed.

Mark 1:34
and Jesus healed many who had various diseases. He also drove out many **demon**s, but he would not let the **demon**s speak because they knew who he was.

Mark 1:39
So he traveled throughout Galilee, preaching in their synagogues and driving out **demon**s.

Mark 3:15
and to have authority to drive out **demon**s.

Mark 3:22
And the teachers of the law who came down from Jerusalem said, "He is possessed by Beelzebul! By the prince of **demon**s he is driving out **demon**s."

Mark 5:1
[*Jesus Restores a **Demon**-Possessed Man*] They went across the lake to the region of the Gerasenes.

Mark 5:12
The **demon**s begged Jesus, "Send us among the pigs; allow us to go into them."

Mark 5:15
When they came to Jesus, they saw the man who had been possessed by the legion of **demon**s, sitting there, dressed and in his right mind; and they were afraid.

Mark 5:16
Those who had seen it told the people what had happened to the **demon**-possessed man—and told about the pigs as well.

Mark 5:18
As Jesus was getting into the boat, the man who had been **demon**-possessed begged to go with him.

Mark 6:13
They drove out many **demon**s and anointed many sick people with oil and healed them.

Mark 7:26
The woman was a Greek, born in Syrian Phoenicia. She begged Jesus to drive the **demon** out of her daughter.

Mark 7:29
Then he told her, "For such a reply, you may go; the **demon** has left your daughter."

Mark 7:30
She went home and found her child lying on the bed, and the **demon** gone.

Mark 9:38
[*Whoever Is Not Against Us Is for Us*] "Teacher," said John, "we saw someone driving out **demon**s in your name and we told him to stop, because he was not one of us."

Mark 16:9
[The earliest manuscripts and some other ancient witnesses do not have verses 9–20.] *When Jesus rose early on the first day of the week, he appeared first to Mary Magdalene, out of whom he had driven seven **demon**s.*

Mark 16:17
*And these signs will accompany those who believe: In my name they will drive
out demons; they will speak in new tongues;*

Luke 4:33
In the synagogue there was a man possessed by a **demon**, an impure spirit. He cried
out at the top of his voice,

Luke 4:35
"Be quiet!" Jesus said sternly. "Come out of him!" Then the **demon** threw the man
down before them all and came out without injuring him.

Luke 4:41
Moreover, **demon**s came out of many people, shouting, "You are the Son of God!" But
he rebuked them and would not allow them to speak, because they knew he was the
Messiah.

Luke 7:33
For John the Baptist came neither eating bread nor drinking wine, and you say, 'He has
a **demon**.'

Luke 8:2
and also some women who had been cured of evil spirits and diseases: Mary (called
Magdalene) from whom seven **demon**s had come out;

Luke 8:26
[*Jesus Restores a **Demon**-Possessed Man*] They sailed to the region of the Gerasenes,
which is across the lake from Galilee.

Luke 8:27
When Jesus stepped ashore, he was met by a **demon**-possessed man from the town.
For a long time this man had not worn clothes or lived in a house, but had lived in the
tombs.

Luke 8:29
For Jesus had commanded the impure spirit to come out of the man. Many times it had
seized him, and though he was chained hand and foot and kept under guard, he had
broken his chains and had been driven by the **demon** into solitary places.

Luke 8:30
Jesus asked him, "What is your name?" "Legion," he replied, because many **demon**s
had gone into him.

Luke 8:32
A large herd of pigs was feeding there on the hillside. The **demon**s begged Jesus to let them go into the pigs, and he gave them permission.

Luke 8:33
When the **demon**s came out of the man, they went into the pigs, and the herd rushed down the steep bank into the lake and was drowned.

Luke 8:35
and the people went out to see what had happened. When they came to Jesus, they found the man from whom the **demon**s had gone out, sitting at Jesus' feet, dressed and in his right mind; and they were afraid.

Luke 8:36
Those who had seen it told the people how the **demon**-possessed man had been cured.

Luke 8:38
The man from whom the **demon**s had gone out begged to go with him, but Jesus sent him away, saying,

Luke 9:1
[*Jesus Sends Out the Twelve*] When Jesus had called the Twelve together, he gave them power and authority to drive out all **demon**s and to cure diseases,

Luke 9:37
[*Jesus Heals a **Demon**-Possessed Boy*] The next day, when they came down from the mountain, a large crowd met him.

Luke 9:42
Even while the boy was coming, the **demon** threw him to the ground in a convulsion. But Jesus rebuked the impure spirit, healed the boy and gave him back to his father.

Luke 9:49
"Master," said John, "we saw someone driving out **demon**s in your name and we tried to stop him, because he is not one of us."

Luke 10:17
The seventy-two returned with joy and said, "Lord, even the **demon**s submit to us in your name."

Luke 11:14
[*Jesus and Beelzebul*] Jesus was driving out a **demon** that was mute. When the **demon** left, the man who had been mute spoke, and the crowd was amazed.

Luke 11:15
But some of them said, "By Beelzebul, the prince of **demon**s, he is driving out **demon**s."

Luke 11:18
If Satan is divided against himself, how can his kingdom stand? I say this because you claim that I drive out **demon**s by Beelzebul.

Luke 11:19
Now if I drive out **demon**s by Beelzebul, by whom do your followers drive them out? So then, they will be your judges.

Luke 11:20
But if I drive out **demon**s by the finger of God, then the kingdom of God has come upon you.

Luke 13:32
He replied, "Go tell that fox, 'I will keep on driving out **demon**s and healing people today and tomorrow, and on the third day I will reach my goal.'
In Context | Full Chapter | Other Translations
John 7:20
"You are **demon**-possessed," the crowd answered. "Who is trying to kill you?"

John 8:48
[*Jesus' Claims About Himself*] The Jews answered him, "Aren't we right in saying that you are a Samaritan and **demon**-possessed?"

John 8:49
"I am not possessed by a **demon**," said Jesus, "but I honor my Father and you dishonor me.

John 8:52
At this they exclaimed, "Now we know that you are **demon**-possessed! Abraham died and so did the prophets, yet you say that whoever obeys your word will never taste death.

John 10:20
Many of them said, "He is **demon**-possessed and raving mad. Why listen to him?"

John 10:21
But others said, "These are not the sayings of a man possessed by a **demon**. Can a **demon** open the eyes of the blind?"

Acts 19:13
Some Jews who went around driving out evil spirits tried to invoke the name of the Lord Jesus over those who were **demon**-possessed. They would say, "In the name of the Jesus whom Paul preaches, I command you to come out."

Romans 8:38
For I am convinced that neither death nor life, neither angels nor **demon**s, neither the present nor the future, nor any powers,

1 Corinthians 10:20
No, but the sacrifices of pagans are offered to **demon**s, not to God, and I do not want you to be participants with **demon**s.

1 Corinthians 10:21
You cannot drink the cup of the Lord and the cup of **demon**s too; you cannot have a part in both the Lord's table and the table of **demon**s.

1 Timothy 4:1
The Spirit clearly says that in later times some will abandon the faith and follow deceiving spirits and things taught by **demon**s.

James 2:19
You believe that there is one God. Good! Even the **demon**s believe that—and shudder.

James 3:15
Such "wisdom" does not come down from heaven but is earthly, unspiritual, **demon**ic.

Revelation 9:20
The rest of mankind who were not killed by these plagues still did not repent of the work of their hands; they did not stop worshiping **demon**s, and idols of gold, silver, bronze, stone and wood—idols that cannot see or hear or walk.

Revelation 16:14
They are **demon**ic spirits that perform signs, and they go out to the kings of the whole world, to gather them for the battle on the great day of God Almighty.

Revelation 18:2
With a mighty voice he shouted: "'Fallen! Fallen is Babylon the Great!' She has become a dwelling for **demon**s and a haunt for every impure spirit, a haunt for every unclean bird, a haunt for every unclean and detestable animal.

Bible Passages: *Body, Heart, Mind, Soul, Spirit* Couplets (100 passages)

Heart and Soul =   30 passages   [0 neg;   0%]

Heart and Spirit -   28 passages   [12 neg; 38%]

Heart and Mind =   20 passages   [8 neg;   40%]

Heart and Body =   6 passages   [3 neg: 50%]

Body and Spirit =   13 passages   [4 neg; 31%]

Mind and Spirit =   9 passages   [5 neg; 56%]

Soul and Spirit =   3 passages   [2 neg: 66%]

Body and Soul =   5 passages   [4 neg; 80%]

Body and Mind =   1 passages   [1 neg; 100%]

Soul and ???? =   37 Total passages   [6 neg: 16%]

Heart and ????   =   80 Total passages   [23 neg: 29%]

Spirit and ????   =   53 Total passages   [21 neg: 40%]

Body and ????   =   25 Total passages   [11 neg: 44%]

Mind and ????   =   30 Total passages   [14 neg: 47%]

Heart and Soul (30 passages)

Deuteronomy 4:29
But if from there you seek the Lord your God, you will find him if you seek him **with all your heart and with all your soul**.

Deuteronomy 6:5
Love the Lord your God with **all your heart and with all your soul and with all your strength**.

Deuteronomy 10:12
[*Fear the Lord*] And now, Israel, what does the Lord your God ask of you but to fear the Lord your God, to walk in obedience to him, to love him, to serve the Lord your God **with all your heart and with all your soul**,

Deuteronomy 11:13
So if you faithfully obey the commands I am giving you today—to love the Lord your God and to serve him **with all your heart and with all your soul**—

Deuteronomy 13:3
you must not listen to the words of that prophet or dreamer. The Lord your God is testing you to find out whether you love him **with all your heart and with all your soul**.

Deuteronomy 26:16
[*Follow the Lord's Commands*] The Lord your God commands you this day to follow these decrees and laws; carefully observe them **with all your heart and with all your soul**.

Deuteronomy 30:2
and when you and your children return to the Lord your God and obey him **with all your heart and with all your soul** according to everything I command you today,

Deuteronomy 30:6
The Lord your God will circumcise your hearts and the hearts of your descendants, so that you may love him **with all your heart and with all your soul**, and live.

Deuteronomy 30:10
if you obey the Lord your God and keep his commands and decrees that are written in this Book of the Law and turn to the Lord your God with all your heart and with all your **soul**.

Joshua 22:5
But be very careful to keep the commandment and the law that Moses the servant of the Lord gave you: to love the Lord your God, to walk in obedience to him, to keep his commands, to hold fast to him and to serve him with all your heart and with all your **soul**."

Joshua 23:14
"Now I am about to go the way of all the earth. You know with all your heart and **soul** that not one of all the good promises the Lord your God gave you has failed. Every promise has been fulfilled; not one has failed.

1 Samuel 14:7
"Do all that you have in mind," his armor-bearer said. "Go ahead; I am **with you heart and soul**."

1 Kings 2:4
and that the Lord may keep his promise to me: 'If your descendants watch how they live, and if they walk faithfully before me **with all their heart and soul**, you will never fail to have a successor on the throne of Israel.'

1 Kings 8:48
and if they turn back to you **with all their heart and soul** in the land of their enemies who took them captive, and pray to you toward the land you gave their ancestors, toward the city you have chosen and the temple I have built for your Name;

2 Kings 23:3
The king stood by the pillar and renewed the covenant in the presence of the Lord—to follow the Lord and keep his commands, statutes and decrees **with all his heart and all his soul**, thus confirming the words of the covenant written in this book. Then all the people pledged themselves to the covenant.

2 Kings 23:25
Neither before nor after Josiah was there a king like him who turned to the Lord as he did—**with all his heart and with all his soul and with all his strength**, in accordance with all the Law of Moses.

1 Chronicles 22:19
Now **devote your heart and soul** to seeking the Lord your God. Begin to build the sanctuary of the Lord God, so that you may bring the ark of the covenant of the Lord and the sacred articles belonging to God into the temple that will be built for the Name of the Lord."

2 Chronicles 6:38
and if they turn back to you **with all their heart and soul** in the land of their captivity where they were taken, and pray toward the land you gave their ancestors, toward the city you have chosen and toward the temple I have built for your Name;

2 Chronicles 15:12
They entered into a covenant to seek the Lord, the God of their ancestors, **with all their heart and soul.**

2 Chronicles 34:31
The king stood by his pillar and renewed the covenant in the presence of the Lord—to follow the Lord and keep his commands, statutes and decrees **with all his heart and all his soul**, and to obey the words of the covenant written in this book.

Psalm 84:2
My **soul yearns**, even faints, for the courts of the Lord; **my heart and my flesh cry out** for the living God.

Psalm 108:1
[*Psalm 108*] [*A song. A psalm of David.*] My **heart**, O God, is steadfast; I will sing and make music with all my **soul**.

Proverbs 2:10
For wisdom **will enter your heart**, and knowledge **will be pleasant to your soul**.

Jeremiah 32:41
I will rejoice in doing them good and will assuredly plant them in this land **with all my heart and soul.**

Matthew 11:29
Take my yoke upon you and learn from me, for **I am gentle and humble in heart, and you will find rest for your souls.**

Matthew 22:37
Jesus replied: "'Love the Lord your God **with all your heart and with all your soul** and with all your mind.'

Mark 12:30
Love the Lord your God **with all your heart and with all your soul** and with all your mind and with all your strength.'

Luke 2:35
so that the thoughts of many **heart**s will be revealed. And a sword will pierce your own **soul** too."

Luke 10:27
He answered, "'Love the Lord your God **with all your heart and with all your soul** and with all your strength and with all your mind'; and, 'Love your neighbor as yourself.'"

Hebrews 4:12
For the word of God is alive and active. Sharper than any double-edged sword, it penetrates even to dividing **soul** and spirit, joints and marrow; it judges the thoughts and attitudes of the **heart**.

Spirit of God (31 of 100)

Genesis 1:2
Now the earth was formless and empty, darkness was over the surface **of** the deep, and the **Spirit of God** was hovering over the waters.

Genesis 41:38
So Pharaoh asked them, "Can we find anyone like this man, one in whom is the **spirit of God**?"

Exodus 31:3
and I have filled him with the **Spirit of God**, with wisdom, with understanding, with knowledge and with all kinds **of** skills—

Exodus 35:31
and he has filled him with the **Spirit of God**, with wisdom, with understanding, with knowledge and with all kinds **of** skills—

Numbers 24:2
When Balaam looked out and saw Israel encamped tribe by tribe, the **Spirit of God** came on him

Deuteronomy 2:30
But Sihon king **of** Heshbon refused to let us pass through. For the Lord your **God** had made his **spirit** stubborn and his heart obstinate in order to give him into your hands, as he has now done.

1 Samuel 10:10
When he and his servant arrived at Gibeah, a procession **of** prophets met him; the **Spirit of God** came powerfully upon him, and he joined in their prophesying.

1 Samuel 11:6
When Saul heard their words, the **Spirit of God** came powerfully upon him, and he burned with anger.

1 Samuel 19:20
so he sent men to capture him. But when they saw a group **of** prophets prophesying, with Samuel standing there as their leader, the **Spirit of God** came on Saul's men, and they also prophesied.

1 Samuel 19:23
So Saul went to Naioth at Ramah. But the **Spirit of God** came even on him, and he walked along prophesying until he came to Naioth.

1 Samuel 30:6
David was greatly distressed because the men were talking **of** stoning him; each one was bitter in **spirit** because **of** his sons and daughters. But David found strength in the Lord his **God**.

2 Kings 23:24
Furthermore, Josiah got rid **of** the mediums and **spirit**ists, the household **god**s, the idols and all the other detestable things seen in Judah and Jerusalem. This he did to fulfill the requirements **of** the law written in the book that Hilkiah the priest had discovered in the temple **of** the Lord.

1 Chronicles 5:26
So the **God of** Israel stirred up the **spirit of** Pul king **of** Assyria (that is, Tiglath-Pileser king **of** Assyria), who took the Reubenites, the Gadites and the half-tribe **of** Manasseh into exile. He took them to Halah, Habor, Hara and the river **of** Gozan, where they are to this day.

1 Chronicles 12:18
Then the **Spirit** came on Amasai, chief **of** the Thirty, and he said: "We are yours, David! We are with you, son **of** Jesse! Success, success to you, and success to those who help you, for your **God** will help you." So David received them and made them leaders **of** his raiding bands.

1 Chronicles 28:12
He gave him the plans **of** all that the **Spirit** had put in his mind for the courts **of** the temple **of** the Lord and all the surrounding rooms, for the treasuries **of** the temple **of God** and for the treasuries for the dedicated things.

2 Chronicles 15:1
[*Asa's Reform*] The **Spirit of God** came on Azariah son **of** Oded.

2 Chronicles 24:20
Then the **Spirit of God** came on Zechariah son **of** Jehoiada the priest. He stood before the people and said, "This is what **God** says: 'Why do you disobey the Lord's commands? You will not prosper. Because you have forsaken the Lord, he has forsaken you.'"

Job 6:4
The arrows **of** the Almighty are in me, my **spirit** drinks in their poison; **God**'s terrors are marshaled against me.

Job 33:4
The **Spirit of God** has made me; the breath **of** the Almighty gives me life.

Psalm 106:33
for they rebelled against the **Spirit of God**, and rash words came from Moses' lips.

Isaiah 8:19
[*The Darkness Turns to Light*] When someone tells you to consult mediums
and **spirit**ists, who whisper and mutter, should not a people inquire **of** their **God**? Why
consult the dead on behalf **of** the living?

Ezekiel 8:3
He stretched out what looked like a hand and took me by the hair **of** my head.
The **Spirit** lifted me up between earth and heaven and in visions **of God** he took me to
Jerusalem, to the entrance **of** the north gate **of** the inner court, where the idol that
provokes to jealousy stood.

Ezekiel 11:1
[*God's Sure Judgment on Jerusalem*] Then the **Spirit** lifted me up and brought me to
the gate **of**the house **of** the Lord that faces east. There at the entrance **of** the gate were
twenty-five men, and I saw among them Jaazaniah son **of** Azzur and Pelatiah
son **of** Benaiah, leaders **of** the people.

Ezekiel 11:24
The **Spirit** lifted me up and brought me to the exiles in Babylonia in the vision given by
the **Spirit of God**. Then the vision I had seen went up from me,

Daniel 4:8
Finally, Daniel came into my presence and I told him the dream. (He is called
Belteshazzar, after the name **of** my **god**, and the **spirit of** the holy **god**s is in him.)

Daniel 4:9
I said, "Belteshazzar, chief **of** the magicians, I know that the **spirit of** the holy **god**s is in
you, and no mystery is too difficult for you. Here is my dream; interpret it for me.

Daniel 4:18
"This is the dream that I, King Nebuchadnezzar, had. Now, Belteshazzar, tell me what it
means, for none **of** the wise men in my kingdom can interpret it for me. But you can,
because the **spirit of** the holy **god**s is in you."

Daniel 5:11
There is a man in your kingdom who has the **spirit of** the holy **god**s in him. In the
time **of** your father he was found to have insight and intelligence and wisdom like
that **of** the **god**s. Your father, King Nebuchadnezzar, appointed him chief **of** the
magicians, enchanters, astrologers and diviners.

Daniel 5:14
I have heard that the **spirit of** the **god**s is in you and that you have insight, intelligence and outstanding wisdom.

Hosea 4:12
My people consult a wooden idol, and a diviner's rod speaks to them.
A **spirit of** prostitution leads them astray; they are unfaithful to their **God**.

Hosea 5:4
"Their deeds do not permit them to return to their **God**. A **spirit of** prostitution is in their heart; they do not acknowledge the Lord.

Haggai 1:14
So the Lord stirred up the **spirit of** Zerubbabel son **of** Shealtiel, governor **of** Judah, and the **spirit of** Joshua son **of** Jozadak, the high priest, and the **spirit of** the whole remnant **of** the people. They came and began to work on the
house **of** the Lord Almighty, their **God**,

Malachi 2:15
Has not the one **God** made you? You belong to him in body and **spirit**. And what does the one **God** seek? **God**ly **of**fspring. So be on your guard, and do not be unfaithful to the wife **of** your youth.

Matthew 3:16
As soon as Jesus was baptized, he went up out **of** the water. At that moment heaven was opened, and he saw the **Spirit of God** descending like a dove and alighting on him.

Matthew 12:28
But if it is by the **Spirit of God** that I drive out demons, then the kingdom **of God** has come upon you.

Mark 3:11
Whenever the impure **spirit**s saw him, they fell down before him and cried out, "You are the Son **of God**."

Luke 1:35
The angel answered, "The Holy **Spirit** will come on you, and the power **of** the Most High will overshadow you. So the holy one to be born will be called the Son **of God**.

John 3:5
Jesus answered, "Very truly I tell you, no one can enter the kingdom **of God** unless they are born **of** water and the **Spirit**.

John 3:34
For the one whom **God** has sent speaks the words **of God**, for **God** gives the **Spirit** without limit.

Acts 2:33
Exalted to the right hand **of God**, he has received from the Father the promised Holy **Spirit** and has poured out what you now see and hear.

Acts 4:31
After they prayed, the place where they were meeting was shaken. And they were all filled with the Holy **Spirit** and spoke the word **of God** boldly.

Acts 5:32
We are witnesses **of** these things, and so is the Holy **Spirit**, whom **God** has given to those who obey him."

Acts 7:55
But Stephen, full **of** the Holy **Spirit**, looked up to heaven and saw the glory **of God**, and Jesus standing at the right hand **of God**.

Acts 10:38
how **God** anointed Jesus **of** Nazareth with the Holy **Spirit** and power, and how he went around doing good and healing all who were under the power **of** the devil, because **God** was with him.

Acts 20:28
Keep watch over yourselves and all the flock **of** which the Holy **Spirit** has made you overseers. Be shepherds **of** the church **of God**, which he bought with his own blood.

Romans 1:4
and who through the **Spirit of** holiness was appointed the Son **of God** in power by his resurrection from the dead: Jesus Christ our Lord.

Romans 1:9
God, whom I serve in my **spirit** in preaching the gospel **of** his Son, is my witness how constantly I remember you

Romans 2:29
No, a person is a Jew who is one inwardly; and circumcision is circumcision **of** the heart, by the **Spirit**, not by the written code. Such a person's praise is not from other people, but from **God**.

Romans 8:9
You, however, are not in the realm **of** the flesh but are in the realm **of** the **Spirit**, if indeed the **Spirit of God** lives in you. And if anyone does not have the **Spirit of** Christ, they do not belong to Christ.

Romans 8:14
For those who are led by the **Spirit of God** are the children **of God**.

Romans 8:27
And he who searches our hearts knows the mind **of** the **Spirit**, because
the **Spirit** intercedes for **God**'s people in accordance with the will **of God**.

Romans 11:8
as it is written: "**God** gave them a **spirit of** stupor, eyes that could not see and ears that
could not hear, to this very day."

Romans 14:17
For the kingdom **of God** is not a matter **of** eating and drinking, but **of** righteousness,
peace and joy in the Holy **Spirit**,

Romans 15:13
May the **God of** hope fill you with all joy and peace as you trust in him, so that you may
overflow with hope by the power **of** the Holy **Spirit**.

Romans 15:16
to be a minister **of** Christ Jesus to the Gentiles. He gave me the priestly
duty **of** proclaiming the gospel **of God**, so that the Gentiles might become an **off**ering
acceptable to **God**, sanctified by the Holy **Spirit**.

Romans 15:19
by the power **of** signs and wonders, through the power **of** the **Spirit of God**. So from
Jerusalem all the way around to Illyricum, I have fully proclaimed the gospel **of** Christ.

Romans 15:30
I urge you, brothers and sisters, by our Lord Jesus Christ and by the love **of** the **Spirit**,
to join me in my struggle by praying to **God** for me.

1 Corinthians 2:6
[*God's Wisdom Revealed by the Spirit*] We do, however, speak a message **of** wisdom
among the mature, but not the wisdom **of** this age or **of** the rulers **of** this age, who are
coming to nothing.

1 Corinthians 2:10
these are the things **God** has revealed to us by his **Spirit**. The **Spirit** searches all things,
even the deep things **of God**.

1 Corinthians 2:11
For who knows a person's thoughts except their own **spirit** within them? In the same
way no one knows the thoughts **of God** except the **Spirit of God**.

1 Corinthians 2:12
What we have received is not the **spirit of** the world, but the **Spirit** who is from **God**, so that we may understand what **God** has freely given us.

1 Corinthians 2:14
The person without the **Spirit** does not accept the things that come from the **Spirit of God** but considers them foolishness, and cannot understand them because they are discerned only through the **Spirit**.

1 Corinthians 6:11
And that is what some **of** you were. But you were washed, you were sanctified, you were justified in the name **of** the Lord Jesus Christ and by the **Spirit of** our **God**.

1 Corinthians 6:19
Do you not know that your bodies are temples **of** the Holy **Spirit**, who is in you, whom you have received from **God**? You are not your own;

1 Corinthians 7:40
In my judgment, she is happier if she stays as she is—and I think that I too have the **Spirit of God**.

1 Corinthians 12:3
Therefore I want you to know that no one who is speaking by the **Spirit of God** says, "Jesus be cursed," and no one can say, "Jesus is Lord," except by the Holy **Spirit**.

1 Corinthians 14:16
Otherwise when you are praising **God** in the **Spirit**, how can someone else, who is now put in the position **of** an inquirer, say "Amen" to your thanksgiving, since they do not know what you are saying?

2 Corinthians 3:3
You show that you are a letter from Christ, the result **of** our ministry, written not with ink but with the **Spirit of** the living **God**, not on tablets **of** stone but on tablets **of** human hearts.

2 Corinthians 7:1
Therefore, since we have these promises, dear friends, let us purify ourselves from everything that contaminates body and **spirit**, perfecting holiness out **of** reverence for **God**.

2 Corinthians 13:14
May the grace **of** the Lord Jesus Christ, and the love **of God**, and the fellowship **of** the Holy **Spirit** be with you all.

Galatians 3:5
So again I ask, does **God** give you his **Spirit** and work miracles among you by the works **of** the law, or by your believing what you heard?

Galatians 4:6
Because you are his sons, **God** sent the **Spirit of** his Son into our hearts, the **Spirit** who calls out, *"Abba*, Father."

Ephesians 1:3
[*Praise for **Spirit**ual Blessings in Christ*] Praise be to the **God** and Father **of** our Lord Jesus Christ, who has blessed us in the heavenly realms with every **spirit**ual blessing in Christ.

Ephesians 1:17
I keep asking that the **God of** our Lord Jesus Christ, the glorious Father, may give you the **Spirit of** wisdom and revelation, so that you may know him better.

Ephesians 4:30
And do not grieve the Holy **Spirit of God**, with whom you were sealed for the day **of** redemption.

Ephesians 6:17
Take the helmet **of** salvation and the sword **of** the **Spirit**, which is the word **of God**.

Philippians 1:19
for I know that through your prayers and **God**'s provision **of** the **Spirit of** Jesus Christ what has happened to me will turn out for my deliverance.

Colossians 1:9
For this reason, since the day we heard about you, we have not stopped praying for you. We continually ask **God** to fill you with the knowledge **of** his will through all the wisdom and understanding that the **Spirit** gives,

Colossians 3:16
Let the message **of** Christ dwell among you richly as you teach and admonish one another with all wisdom through psalms, hymns, and songs from the **Spirit**, singing to **God** with gratitude in your hearts.

1 Thessalonians 5:23
May **God** himself, the **God of** peace, sanctify you through and through. May your whole **spirit**, soul and body be kept blameless at the coming **of** our Lord Jesus Christ.

2 Thessalonians 2:13
[*Stand Firm*] But we ought always to thank **God** for you, brothers and sisters loved by the Lord, because **God** chose you as first fruits to be saved through the sanctifying work **of** the **Spirit** and through belief in the truth.

Hebrews 2:4
God also testified to it by signs, wonders and various miracles, and by gifts **of** the Holy **Spirit** distributed according to his will.

Hebrews 4:12
For the word **of God** is alive and active. Sharper than any double-edged sword, it penetrates even to dividing soul and **spirit**, joints and marrow; it judges the thoughts and attitudes **of** the heart.

Hebrews 9:14
How much more, then, will the blood **of** Christ, who through the eternal **Spirit of**fered himself unblemished to **God**, cleanse our consciences from acts that lead to death, so that we may serve the living **God**!

Hebrews 10:29
How much more severely do you think someone deserves to be punished who has trampled the Son **of God** underfoot, who has treated as an unholy thing the blood **of** the covenant that sanctified them, and who has insulted the **Spirit of** grace?

Hebrews 12:23
to the church **of** the firstborn, whose names are written in heaven. You have come to **God**, the Judge **of** all, to the **spirit**s **of** the righteous made perfect,

1 Peter 1:2
who have been chosen according to the foreknowledge **of God** the Father, through the sanctifying work **of** the **Spirit**, to be obedient to Jesus Christ and sprinkled with his blood: Grace and peace be yours in abundance.

1 Peter 2:5
you also, like living stones, are being built into a **spirit**ual house to be a holy priesthood, **of**fering **spirit**ual sacrifices acceptable to **God** through Jesus Christ.

1 Peter 3:4
Rather, it should be that **of** your inner self, the unfading beauty **of** a gentle and quiet **spirit**, which is **of** great worth in **God**'s sight.

1 Peter 4:14
If you are insulted because **of** the name **of** Christ, you are blessed, for the **Spirit of** glory and **of God** rests on you.

1 John 4:2
This is how you can recognize the **Spirit of God**: Every **spirit** that acknowledges that Jesus Christ has come in the flesh is from **God**,

1 John 4:3
but every **spirit** that does not acknowledge Jesus is not from **God**. This is the **spirit of** the antichrist, which you have heard is coming and even now is already in the world.

1 John 4:6
We are from **God**, and whoever knows **God** listens to us; but whoever is not from **God** does not listen to us. This is how we recognize the **Spirit of** truth and the **spirit of** falsehood.

Revelation 2:7
Whoever has ears, let them hear what the **Spirit** says to the churches. To the one who is victorious, I will give the right to eat from the tree **of** life, which is in the paradise **of God**.

Revelation 3:1
[*To the Church in Sardis*] "To the angel **of** the church in Sardis write: These are the words **of** him who holds the seven **spirits of God** and the seven stars. I know your deeds; you have a reputation **of** being alive, but you are dead.

Revelation 4:5
From the throne came flashes **of** lightning, rumblings and peals **of** thunder. In front **of** the throne, seven lamps were blazing. These are the seven **spirits of God**.

Revelation 5:6
Then I saw a Lamb, looking as if it had been slain, standing at the center **of** the throne, encircled by the four living creatures and the elders. The Lamb had seven horns and seven eyes, which are the seven **spirits of God** sent out into all the earth.

Revelation 16:14
They are demonic **spirits** that perform signs, and they go out to the kings **of** the whole world, to gather them for the battle on the great day **of God** Almighty.

Revelation 19:10
At this I fell at his feet to worship him. But he said to me, "Don't do that! I am a fellow servant with you and with your brothers and sisters who hold to the testimony **of** Jesus. Worship **God**! For it is the **Spirit of** prophecy who bears testimony to Jesus."

Revelation 21:10

And he carried me away in the **Spirit** to a mountain great and high, and showed me the Holy City, Jerusalem, coming down out **of** heaven from **God**.

Spirit of Jesus Christ (2 of 20)

Acts 2:38
Peter replied, "Repent and be baptized, every one **of** you, in the
name **of Jesus Christ** for the forgiveness **of** your sins. And you will receive the
gift **of** the Holy **Spirit**.

Acts 16:18
She kept this up for many days. Finally Paul became so annoyed that he turned around
and said to the **spirit**, "In the name **of Jesus Christ** I command you to come out **of** her!"
At that moment the **spirit** left her.

Romans 1:4
and who through the **Spirit of** holiness was appointed the Son **of** God in power by his
resurrection from the dead: **Jesus Christ** our Lord.

Romans 8:2
because through **Christ Jesus** the law **of** the **Spirit** who gives life has set you free from
the law **of** sin and death.

Romans 8:11
And if the **Spirit of** him who raised **Jesus** from the dead is living in you, he who
raised **Christ** from the dead will also give life to your mortal bodies
because **of** his **Spirit** who lives in you.

Romans 15:16
to be a minister **of Christ Jesus** to the Gentiles. He gave me the priestly
duty **of** proclaiming the gospel **of** God, so that the Gentiles might become an **of**fering
acceptable to God, sanctified by the Holy **Spirit**.

Romans 15:30
I urge you, brothers and sisters, by our Lord **Jesus Christ** and by the love **of** the **Spirit**,
to join me in my struggle by praying to God for me.

1 Corinthians 6:11
And that is what some **of** you were. But you were washed, you were sanctified, you
were justified in the name **of** the Lord **Jesus Christ** and by the **Spirit of** our God.

2 Corinthians 13:14
May the grace **of** the Lord **Jesus Christ**, and the love **of** God, and the fellowship **of** the
Holy **Spirit** be with you all.

Galatians 3:14
He redeemed us in order that the blessing given to Abraham might come to the Gentiles through **Christ Jesus**, so that by faith we might receive the promise **of** the **Spirit**.

Galatians 6:18
The grace **of** our Lord **Jesus Christ** be with your **spirit**, brothers and sisters. Amen.

Ephesians 1:3
[*Praise for Spiritual Blessings in Christ*] Praise be to the God and Father **of** our Lord **Jesus Christ**, who has blessed us in the heavenly realms with every **spirit**ual blessing in **Christ**.

Ephesians 1:17
I keep asking that the God **of** our Lord **Jesus Christ**, the glorious Father, may give you the **Spirit of** wisdom and revelation, so that you may know him better.

Philippians 1:19
for I know that through your prayers and God's provision **of** the **Spirit of Jesus Christ** what has happened to me will turn out for my deliverance.

Philippians 4:23
The grace **of** the Lord **Jesus Christ** be with your **spirit**. Amen.

1 Thessalonians 5:23
May God himself, the God **of** peace, sanctify you through and through. May your whole **spirit**, soul and body be kept blameless at the coming **of** our Lord **Jesus Christ**.

Philemon 1:25
The grace **of** the Lord **Jesus Christ** be with your **spirit**.

1 Peter 1:2
who have been chosen according to the foreknowledge **of** God the Father, through the sanctifying work **of** the **Spirit**, to be obedient to **Jesus Christ** and sprinkled with his blood: Grace and peace be yours in abundance.

1 Peter 2:5
you also, like living stones, are being built into a **spirit**ual house to be a holy priesthood, **of**fering **spirit**ual sacrifices acceptable to God through **Jesus Christ**.

1 John 4:2
This is how you can recognize the **Spirit of** God: Every **spirit** that acknowledges that **Jesus Christ** has come in the flesh is from God,

<u>Holy Spirit (104)</u>
(Gospels – 27, Acts through Revelation – 65; NT Total = 92)

Psalm 51:11
Do not cast me from your presence or take your **Holy Spirit** from me.

Isaiah 57:15
For this is what the high and exalted One says— he who lives forever, whose name is **holy**: "I live in a high and **holy** place, but also with the one who is contrite and lowly in **spirit**, to revive the **spirit** of the lowly and to revive the heart of the contrite.

Isaiah 63:10
Yet they rebelled and grieved his **Holy Spirit**. So he turned and became their enemy and he himself fought against them.

Isaiah 63:11
Then his people recalled the days of old, the days of Moses and his people— where is he who brought them through the sea, with the shepherd of his flock? Where is he who set his **Holy Spirit** among them,

Daniel 4:8
Finally, Daniel came into my presence and I told him the dream. (He is called Belteshazzar, after the name of my god, and the **spirit** of the **holy** gods is in him.)

Daniel 4:9
I said, "Belteshazzar, chief of the magicians, I know that the **spirit** of the **holy** gods is in you, and no mystery is too difficult for you. Here is my dream; interpret it for me.

Daniel 4:18
"This is the dream that I, King Nebuchadnezzar, had. Now, Belteshazzar, tell me what it means, for none of the wise men in my kingdom can interpret it for me. But you can, because the **spirit** of the **holy** gods is in you."

Daniel 5:11
There is a man in your kingdom who has the **spirit** of the **holy** gods in him. In the time of your father he was found to have insight and intelligence and wisdom like that of the gods. Your father, King Nebuchadnezzar, appointed him chief of the magicians, enchanters, astrologers and diviners.

Matthew 1:18
[*Joseph Accepts Jesus as His Son*] This is how the birth of Jesus the Messiah came about: His mother Mary was pledged to be married to Joseph, but before they came together, she was found to be pregnant through the **Holy Spirit**.

Matthew 1:20
But after he had considered this, an angel of the Lord appeared to him in a dream and said, "Joseph son of David, do not be afraid to take Mary home as your wife, because what is conceived in her is from the **Holy Spirit**.

Matthew 3:11
"I baptize you with water for repentance. But after me comes one who is more powerful than I, whose sandals I am not worthy to carry. He will baptize you with the **Holy Spirit** and fire.

Matthew 12:32
Anyone who speaks a word against the Son of Man will be forgiven, but anyone who speaks against the **Holy Spirit** will not be forgiven, either in this age or in the age to come.

Matthew 28:19
Therefore go and make disciples of all nations, baptizing them in the name of the Father and of the Son and of the **Holy Spirit**,

Mark 1:8
I baptize you with water, but he will baptize you with the **Holy Spirit**."

Mark 3:29
but whoever blasphemes against the **Holy Spirit** will never be forgiven; they are guilty of an eternal sin."

Mark 12:36
David himself, speaking by the **Holy Spirit**, declared: "'The Lord said to my Lord: "Sit at my right hand until I put your enemies under your feet."'

Mark 13:11
Whenever you are arrested and brought to trial, do not worry beforehand about what to say. Just say whatever is given you at the time, for it is not you speaking, but the **Holy Spirit**.

Luke 1:15
for he will be great in the sight of the Lord. He is never to take wine or other fermented drink, and he will be filled with the **Holy Spirit** even before he is born.

Luke 1:35
The angel answered, "The **Holy Spirit** will come on you, and the power of the Most High will overshadow you. So the **holy** one to be born will be called the Son of God.

Luke 1:41
When Elizabeth heard Mary's greeting, the baby leaped in her womb, and Elizabeth was filled with the **Holy Spirit**.

Luke 1:67
[*Zechariah's Song*] His father Zechariah was filled with the **Holy Spirit** and prophesied:

Luke 2:25
Now there was a man in Jerusalem called Simeon, who was righteous and devout. He was waiting for the consolation of Israel, and the **Holy Spirit** was on him.

Luke 2:26
It had been revealed to him by the **Holy Spirit** that he would not die before he had seen the Lord's Messiah.

Luke 3:16
John answered them all, "I baptize you with water. But one who is more powerful than I will come, the straps of whose sandals I am not worthy to untie. He will baptize you with the **Holy Spirit** and fire.

Luke 3:22
and the **Holy Spirit** descended on him in bodily form like a dove. And a voice came from heaven: "You are my Son, whom I love; with you I am well pleased."

Luke 4:1
[*Jesus Is Tested in the Wilderness*] Jesus, full of the **Holy Spirit**, left the Jordan and was led by the **Spirit** into the wilderness,

Luke 10:21
At that time Jesus, full of joy through the **Holy Spirit**, said, "I praise you, Father, Lord of heaven and earth, because you have hidden these things from the wise and learned, and revealed them to little children. Yes, Father, for this is what you were pleased to do.

Luke 11:13
If you then, though you are evil, know how to give good gifts to your children, how much more will your Father in heaven give the **Holy Spirit** to those who ask him!"

Luke 12:10
And everyone who speaks a word against the Son of Man will be forgiven, but anyone who blasphemes against the **Holy Spirit** will not be forgiven.

Luke 12:12
for the **Holy Spirit** will teach you at that time what you should say."

John 1:33
And I myself did not know him, but the one who sent me to baptize with water told me, 'The man on whom you see the **Spirit** come down and remain is the one who will baptize with the **Holy Spirit**.'

John 14:15
[*Jesus Promises the **Holy Spirit***] "If you love me, keep my commands.

John 14:26
But the Advocate, the **Holy Spirit**, whom the Father will send in my name, will teach you all things and will remind you of everything I have said to you.

John 15:26
[*The Work of the **Holy Spirit***] "When the Advocate comes, whom I will send to you from the Father—the **Spirit** of truth who goes out from the Father—he will testify about me.

John 20:22
And with that he breathed on them and said, "Receive the **Holy Spirit**.

Acts 1:2
until the day he was taken up to heaven, after giving instructions through the **Holy Spirit** to the apostles he had chosen.

Acts 1:5
For John baptized with water, but in a few days you will be baptized with the **Holy Spirit**."

Acts 1:8
But you will receive power when the **Holy Spirit** comes on you; and you will be my witnesses in Jerusalem, and in all Judea and Samaria, and to the ends of the earth."

Acts 1:16
and said, "Brothers and sisters, the Scripture had to be fulfilled in which the **Holy Spirit** spoke long ago through David concerning Judas, who served as guide for those who arrested Jesus.

Acts 2:1
[*The **Holy Spirit** Comes at Pentecost*] When the day of Pentecost came, they were all together in one place.

Acts 2:4
All of them were filled with the **Holy Spirit** and began to speak in other tongues as the **Spirit** enabled them.

Acts 2:33
Exalted to the right hand of God, he has received from the Father the promised **Holy Spirit** and has poured out what you now see and hear.

Acts 2:38
Peter replied, "Repent and be baptized, every one of you, in the name of Jesus Christ for the forgiveness of your sins. And you will receive the gift of the **Holy Spirit**.

Acts 4:8
Then Peter, filled with the **Holy Spirit**, said to them: "Rulers and elders of the people!

Acts 4:25
You spoke by the **Holy Spirit** through the mouth of your servant, our father David: "'Why do the nations rage and the peoples plot in vain?

Acts 4:31
After they prayed, the place where they were meeting was shaken. And they were all filled with the **Holy Spirit** and spoke the word of God boldly.

Acts 5:3
Then Peter said, "Ananias, how is it that Satan has so filled your heart that you have lied to the **Holy Spirit** and have kept for yourself some of the money you received for the land?

Acts 5:32
We are witnesses of these things, and so is the **Holy Spirit**, whom God has given to those who obey him."

Acts 6:5
This proposal pleased the whole group. They chose Stephen, a man full of faith and of the **Holy Spirit**; also Philip, Procorus, Nicanor, Timon, Parmenas, and Nicolas from Antioch, a convert to Judaism.

Acts 7:51
"You stiff-necked people! Your hearts and ears are still uncircumcised. You are just like your ancestors: You always resist the **Holy Spirit**!

Acts 7:55
But Stephen, full of the **Holy Spirit**, looked up to heaven and saw the glory of God, and Jesus standing at the right hand of God.

Acts 8:15

When they arrived, they prayed for the new believers there that they might receive the **Holy Spirit**,

Acts 8:16

because the **Holy Spirit** had not yet come on any of them; they had simply been baptized in the name of the Lord Jesus.

Acts 8:17

Then Peter and John placed their hands on them, and they received the **Holy Spirit**.

Acts 8:19

and said, "Give me also this ability so that everyone on whom I lay my hands may receive the **Holy Spirit**."

Acts 9:17

Then Ananias went to the house and entered it. Placing his hands on Saul, he said, "Brother Saul, the Lord—Jesus, who appeared to you on the road as you were coming here—has sent me so that you may see again and be filled with the **Holy Spirit**."

Acts 9:31

Then the church throughout Judea, Galilee and Samaria enjoyed a time of peace and was strengthened. Living in the fear of the Lord and encouraged by the **Holy Spirit**, it increased in numbers.

Acts 10:38

how God anointed Jesus of Nazareth with the **Holy Spirit** and power, and how he went around doing good and healing all who were under the power of the devil, because God was with him.

Acts 10:44

While Peter was still speaking these words, the **Holy Spirit** came on all who heard the message.

Acts 10:45

The circumcised believers who had come with Peter were astonished that the gift of the **Holy Spirit** had been poured out even on Gentiles.

Acts 10:47

"Surely no one can stand in the way of their being baptized with water. They have received the **Holy Spirit** just as we have."

Acts 11:15

"As I began to speak, the **Holy Spirit** came on them as he had come on us at the beginning.

Acts 11:16
Then I remembered what the Lord had said: 'John baptized with water, but you will be baptized with the **Holy Spirit**.'

Acts 11:24
He was a good man, full of the **Holy Spirit** and faith, and a great number of people were brought to the Lord.

Acts 13:2
While they were worshiping the Lord and fasting, the **Holy Spirit** said, "Set apart for me Barnabas and Saul for the work to which I have called them."

Acts 13:4
[*On Cyprus*] The two of them, sent on their way by the **Holy Spirit**, went down to Seleucia and sailed from there to Cyprus.

Acts 13:9
Then Saul, who was also called Paul, filled with the **Holy Spirit**, looked straight at Elymas and said,

Acts 13:52
And the disciples were filled with joy and with the **Holy Spirit**.

Acts 15:8
God, who knows the heart, showed that he accepted them by giving the **Holy Spirit** to them, just as he did to us.

Acts 15:28
It seemed good to the **Holy Spirit** and to us not to burden you with anything beyond the following requirements:

Acts 16:6
[*Paul's Vision of the Man of Macedonia*] Paul and his companions traveled throughout the region of Phrygia and Galatia, having been kept by the **Holy Spirit** from preaching the word in the province of Asia.

Acts 19:2
and asked them, "Did you receive the **Holy Spirit** when you believed?" They answered, "No, we have not even heard that there is a **Holy Spirit**."

Acts 19:6
When Paul placed his hands on them, the **Holy Spirit** came on them, and they spoke in tongues and prophesied.

Acts 20:23

I only know that in every city the **Holy Spirit** warns me that prison and hardships are facing me.

Acts 20:28

Keep watch over yourselves and all the flock of which the **Holy Spirit** has made you overseers. Be shepherds of the church of God, which he bought with his own blood.

Acts 21:11

Coming over to us, he took Paul's belt, tied his own hands and feet with it and said, "The **Holy Spirit** says, 'In this way the Jewish leaders in Jerusalem will bind the owner of this belt and will hand him over to the Gentiles.'"

Acts 28:25

They disagreed among themselves and began to leave after Paul had made this final statement: "The **Holy Spirit** spoke the truth to your ancestors when he said through Isaiah the prophet:

Romans 5:5

And hope does not put us to shame, because God's love has been poured out into our hearts through the **Holy Spirit**, who has been given to us.

Romans 9:1

[*Paul's Anguish Over Israel*] I speak the truth in Christ—I am not lying, my conscience confirms it through the **Holy Spirit**—

Romans 14:17

For the kingdom of God is not a matter of eating and drinking, but of righteousness, peace and joy in the **Holy Spirit**,

Romans 15:13

May the God of hope fill you with all joy and peace as you trust in him, so that you may overflow with hope by the power of the **Holy Spirit**.

Romans 15:16

to be a minister of Christ Jesus to the Gentiles. He gave me the priestly duty of proclaiming the gospel of God, so that the Gentiles might become an offering acceptable to God, sanctified by the **Holy Spirit**.

1 Corinthians 6:19

Do you not know that your bodies are temples of the **Holy Spirit**, who is in you, whom you have received from God? You are not your own;

1 Corinthians 12:3
Therefore I want you to know that no one who is speaking by the **Spirit** of God says, "Jesus be cursed," and no one can say, "Jesus is Lord," except by the **Holy Spirit**.

2 Corinthians 6:6
in purity, understanding, patience and kindness; in the **Holy Spirit** and in sincere love;

2 Corinthians 13:14
May the grace of the Lord Jesus Christ, and the love of God, and the fellowship of the **Holy Spirit** be with you all.

Ephesians 1:13
And you also were included in Christ when you heard the message of truth, the gospel of your salvation. When you believed, you were marked in him with a seal, the promised **Holy Spirit**,

Ephesians 3:5
which was not made known to people in other generations as it has now been revealed by the **Spirit** to God's **holy** apostles and prophets.

Ephesians 4:30
And do not grieve the **Holy Spirit** of God, with whom you were sealed for the day of redemption.

1 Thessalonians 1:5
because our gospel came to you not simply with words but also with power, with the **Holy Spirit** and deep conviction. You know how we lived among you for your sake.

1 Thessalonians 1:6
You became imitators of us and of the Lord, for you welcomed the message in the midst of severe suffering with the joy given by the **Holy Spirit**.

1 Thessalonians 4:8
Therefore, anyone who rejects this instruction does not reject a human being but God, the very God who gives you his **Holy Spirit**.

2 Timothy 1:14
Guard the good deposit that was entrusted to you—guard it with the help of the **Holy Spirit** who lives in us.

Titus 3:5
he saved us, not because of righteous things we had done, but because of his mercy. He saved us through the washing of rebirth and renewal by the **Holy Spirit**,

Hebrews 2:4
God also testified to it by signs, wonders and various miracles, and by gifts of the **Holy Spirit** distributed according to his will.

Hebrews 3:7
[*Warning Against Unbelief*] So, as the **Holy Spirit** says: "Today, if you hear his voice,

Hebrews 6:4
It is impossible for those who have once been enlightened, who have tasted the heavenly gift, who have shared in the **Holy Spirit**,

Hebrews 9:8
The **Holy Spirit** was showing by this that the way into the Most **Holy** Place had not yet been disclosed as long as the first tabernacle was still functioning.

Hebrews 10:15
The **Holy Spirit** also testifies to us about this. First he says:

1 Peter 1:12
It was revealed to them that they were not serving themselves but you, when they spoke of the things that have now been told you by those who have preached the gospel to you by the **Holy Spirit** sent from heaven. Even angels long to look into these things.

1 Peter 2:5
you also, like living stones, are being built into a **spirit**ual house to be a **holy** priesthood, offering **spirit**ual sacrifices acceptable to God through Jesus Christ.

2 Peter 1:21
For prophecy never had its origin in the human will, but prophets, though human, spoke from God as they were carried along by the **Holy Spirit**.

Jude 1:20
But you, dear friends, by building yourselves up in your most **holy** faith and praying in the **Holy Spirit**,

Revelation 21:10
And he carried me away in the **Spirit** to a mountain great and high, and showed me the **Holy** City, Jerusalem, coming down out of heaven from God.

Small Group Process Description

PREPARATION

1. Solicit 4-5 pairs (8-10 individuals) to gather for 10 weeks for this study – the first week being an orientation session, the 8-week study, and the last week being the closing session.
2. Each week participants individually read the 'condensed' passages, the individual passages in the Appendices, and reflect on their meaning.
3. Each week each participant is paired with a different partner. Mid-week the pair meet briefly or have a brief phone conversation about the passages.
4. At the beginning of each gathering, a different participant offers an opening and closing prayer.

PRACTICE

5. To begin each weekly session, each individual takes time to re-read the 'condensed' passages of the week, consider how they are experienced in their life.
6. Each individual sits with his or her partner of this particular week, and each person shares their self-reflections with the other, the pair discusses how they might expand and deepen their experience of the heart (soul, spirit, or Holy Spirit), and then they end the pair-dialogue by choosing something of value to be shared in the large group.
7. When all pairs have finished, the whole group gathers together, and one of each pair represents the pair and briefly shares one or two aspects of most value ('gem') that came out of their pair-dialogue, in turn.
8. After pair-sharing is completed, group conversation begins about what was shared. At the end of group conversation, one participant volunteers to say a prayer aloud to and for the whole group.

PERFORMANCE

9. After the prayer in the whole group, a short period of reflection occurs and then each participant in the circle briefly shares one thing of value – their 'gem' or 'pearl' of the gathering that they are leaving with and that they may try to implement in their lives in a new way.
10. At the end of this sharing one participant offers a prayer and blessing to close the group. By the end of the 10 weeks each participant should have offered the closing benediction, in turn.
11. At the closing session, the group celebrates and considers how they might take what was learned out into the world.
12. Each pairs consider soliciting four new pairs (8 individuals) for another study, forming one to three additional groups.

Small Group Process: *Dialectio Communitas Divina* (80-90 min)

1. Individual Self-reflection: Read scripture passages, meditate, contemplate, pray.

(***Instruct*** ... (*lectio Divina*) recognize, revere & preserve God's Promises within oneself. Believe and love God.)

Still the body, calm the heart, quiet the mind, empty and open. This internal, silent reflection is emptying and opening in order to attend to God speaking through Scripture. See & believe. Hear & Follow.

(10 min reading & considering passages to oneself)

2. Pair-Dialogue: Read aloud to partner, examine, make contrition/repent, pray.

(***Illuminate*** ... reconcile separation & restore relationship with the Lord's Presence and His will for your path in His Plan. Have faith and love one another.)

This refraction with another brother or sister is an examination of my life in order to attach to God's presence and instruction. Feel remorse at failure. Repent. Be forgiven.
(20 min sharing reflections and discussing with partner)

3. Pair-sharing to group: Read aloud to group, share, converse, pray.

(***Inform*** ... reveal & conserve Truth through the Holy Spirit)

This revelation is a seeking and sharing of forgiveness in community (bread and wine). Witness the Word into Works. Share salvation, save souls.

(30 min pairs sharing refractions and whole group conversation)

4. Blessing and Benediction: Convey transformation, pray.

(***Inspire*** ... sanctify & consecrate the Sacred)

This re-composing is finding the comfort and peace of atonement. Die to the world and be re-born to the Kingdom of Heaven. Begin anew.

(15 min each individual sharing with group what 'gem' or 'pearl' they are leaving with)

A One-Year Study of the Gospels *(Fall 2018 through Summer 2019)*

The Little Stories (Parables) of Jesus

9/14 *Light for the World   In the Care of the Father Come as Little Children to Me Prepare to Enter the Kingdom of Heaven*
9/21   *Finding the Treasure*
9/28   *Growing The Treasure*
10/5   *Storing, Securing and Sharing (increasing) the Treasure*
10/12   *Harvesting the Treasure*
10/19   *Seeing and Believing That One is Lost (repent)*
10/26   *Hearing and Understanding the Invitation (surrender)*
11/2   *Finding and Entering the Portal (seek)*
11/9   *Living Through Your Heart Into Your Soul (love)*
11/16   Closing this study ... Orienting to the next study

The Teachings of Jesus

11/30; 12/7 *God gifts His Son (1,2) (3.4)*
12/14;21   *Jesus directs how to receive God's Gift <u>within</u> each person (5,6) (7,8)*
12/21;1/4 *Jesus teaches about relationship <u>between</u> each one and another (9,10) (11,12)*
1/11;18   *Jesus teaches about relations <u>among</u> family, groups & communities (13,14) (15,16)*
1/25; 2/1 *Jesus engages the institutions of man (17,18) (19,20)*
2/8; 15   *Jesus portrays the kingdom of heaven (21,22) (23,24)*
2/22; 3/1 *Jesus demonstrates authority of kingdom of heaven over the institutions of man (25,26;27,28)*
3/8;15   *Jesus rises, returns and begins the Christian church <u>through</u> the Holy Spirit (29,30)*
3/22   Closing this study ... Orienting to the next study

The Holy Spirit

3/29 *Heart*   4/26 *Heart & Soul, Body & Mind*
4/5 *Soul*   5/3 *Spirit of God*
4/12 *Spirit*   5/10 *Holy Spirit*
4/19 *Demons*   5/17 *Concluding Thoughts* (20 NT passages concerning the Spirit of Jesus)
                        5/24 Closing this study ... Orienting to the next study

The Lord's Prayers (The 33 Gospel passages concerning prayer)

6/7   *Pray with patience, perseverance and reverence: Know God's past actions, His plan and His presence*
6/14 *Pray to clear and cleanse a space for the Holy Spirit: Empty and open, be cleansed, be filled*
6/21 *Pray with awareness of God's Love: Love Christ; love your enemy; forgive others; rest in the love of Christ*
6/28 *Pray that each one might receive Christ: express gratitude, have faith, share with the distant & different*
7/12 *Pray to believe that Jesus is the Son of God: dispel unbelief and cleanse us of the darkest evil*
7/19 *Pray for knowledge of God: Promise, Path and Presence*
7/26 *Pray for knowledge of God's Actions: Pardon, Provision and Protection*
8/2   *Fear not, give thanks, and praise the Lord for the gift of eternal life*
8/9   Closing Session

The Little Stories (Parables) of Jesus. Christina and I found that 16 key 'little stories' Jesus told, located in the first half of his ministry, can be arranged thematically in four groups of four parables. An additional 16 parables in the last year of his ministry cluster nicely into four sets of four parables each, as well. Finally, we gathered up the remaining little stories and arranged them in groups of four by theme, and they just seemed to fall into place. On top of that, the 'leftover' stories seemed to introduce everything, outline what was to come in the primary 32 stories of the main study, and then to conclude everything. So we placed these four groups of four leftover stories at the beginning as an orientation to the whole study.

The Teachings of Jesus. The second study uses an integrated chronological Bible and focuses on a four-part pattern we discerned that provides a unique scaffold for studying the four Gospels: It appears that 1) an issue is presented to Jesus; 2) Jesus then allows and/or encourages others to respond to the issue; 3) after which Jesus responds with a different, deeper perspective, involving a significant principle he wishes to teach;   4) which he then demonstrates in action. When this frame is used to partition the Gospels, there appear to be 32 + 1 lessons – sixteen in the first two years of his ministry and sixteen 'lessons' in the last year of his ministry. Each set of sixteen lessons seem to naturally cluster into groups of four that describe a progressive sequence to the teachings of Jesus in a remarkably meaningful manner.

The Holy Spirit. In this study, each week we look separately at all the passages containing the word 'heart' (149), 'soul' (95), 'spirit' (270), 'demon' (76), 'combinations of two or more of these words' (100), 'Spirit of God' (100), 'Holy Spirit' (104), and 'Spirit of Jesus' (20). Damian took the passages, highlighted the key meaningful phrases across all passages, deleted duplication, and arranged the phrases into an organized "condensed version" of a few paragraphs. This study looks at the scriptural relations among heart and soul, body and mind, spirit and Holy Spirit, finding the central position the heart holds as the primary arena wherein evil tries to separate the soul from spirit and the Holy Spirit seeks to bind them into one whole with the Spirit of God.

The Lord's Prayers. We used this 'four by four' scaffold to look at all the passages in the Gospels concerning prayer. We found four initial passages about prayer involving Zechariah, Mary, Simeon and Anna and then 32 passages about prayer of and by Jesus, with a final passage after his resurrection. Again, dividing these prayer passages into the sixteen during the first two years of Jesus' ministry and the sixteen prayer passages during the last year of his ministry, we found that it allowed new and exciting insights: When partitioned into clusters according to our previous studies, the first clusters of sixteen prayer passages clearly define and elaborate the meaning of each line of the "Lord's Prayer", one line at a time. Jesus then repeats his offering of the 'Lord's Prayer' at the beginning of his last year of ministry and in the last clusters of sixteen passages about prayer offers what each person who prays should 'ask, seek and knock for', specifying what Gift each person will then be 'given, find and what will be opened'.

www.ingramcontent.com/pod-product-compliance
Lightning Source LLC
LaVergne TN
LVHW061336060426
835511LV00014B/1942